I0406805

REAL WORLD SELLING STRATEGIES
THE ART OF THE SELLING CONVERSATION

BY HAL THORSVIG & JAMES HAYDEN

Table of Contents

PREFACE

Adapt or die -as my first boss said.

Your world is getting rocked.

Why would anyone want to read another book touting successful selling techniques and how to sell more? Hasn't just about everything that could be written about selling success been written? Or so it would seem, from the volume of available material on bookshelves that suggest how to sell yourself to others, or how to understand a prospect(s)'s reason for buying or determining the decision makers. And it hardly ends here. Every imaginable sales situation has been diagnosed and dissected countless times and numerous approaches to solutions applied. Yet are you any further ahead in your career as a salesperson? How is your close ratio? Are you earning more business or losing more business? Are you and your sales team wasting time trying to follow up on sales that just don't close? How accurate is your sales pipeline?

So, what IS new here? And what would entice someone to purchase another "business success" book?

The world has changed since we published the first edition of this book in 2013. There are several updates and specifically, two new chapters: channel management and technology and the sales professional. McKinsey predicts 45% of all marketing and sales jobs will be replaced by AI. If you are not staying ahead of technology and follow a sales process, you will end up like the buggy whip salesperson in the 1950's. Or like Mr. Brown the bookseller… in a bustling city, there was a street lined with small shops selling all kinds of goods. One of these shops was a small bookstore owned by an old man named Mr. Brown. Mr. Brown had been running his bookstore for over 40 years and had seen many changes in the city.

One day, a new technology emerged that allowed people to read books on electronic devices. This technology quickly became popular, and more and more people started buying e-books instead of physical books. Mr. Brown noticed that fewer and fewer customers were coming into his store.

At first, he tried to adapt by selling e-books in his store, but he soon realized that he couldn't compete with the large online retailers who could offer a wider selection at lower prices. Eventually, Mr. Brown had to close his bookstore.

The street where Mr. Brown's bookstore once stood is now filled with trendy cafes and boutique clothing stores. The old bookstore is just a memory, a reminder of a time before technology changed the way we consume books.

Channel Management: Forrester reports that 75% of all technology sales revenue is through partners. What is prepared is a definitive guide for recruiting and selecting partners, how to onboard the partners and continual, ongoing optimization of the partners.

Technology, whew! My advisory/consulting clients suggested that a section was necessary on technology and today's business development professional. My intention was to research and provide information on the impact of CRM and other sales technology support.

During the past two years I have been utilizing marketing intelligence, campaign management and other sales tracking CRM software. All these tools have improved sales processes and efficiency. Then, I discovered AI and how it's impacted our work today and likely will impact how you approach business. Hang onto your hats, it's going to be a fun ride. The changes and velocity of change is incredible. To keep you as a reader current, we will be offering a twice a month subscription-based technology update for the sales professional. Please see.www.Jamesbhayden.com.

If, as a salesperson you are not following a sales process, like the process in our book, and you are utilizing technology and Artificial Intelligence as tools or your assistants you will get left behind and your probability of living the life you want and being successful in your career will diminish. The world of sales and revenue generation is shifting under your feet. Our objective is to provide a life raft and guide you through the turbulent waters to more business and life success.

Our goal is to dispel past selling myths and ineffective sales techniques that are rampant in the business world and which cost companies millions of dollars of revenue in lost sales and under-performing customers.

Our book is based on the concept that PEOPLE buy. We will give you and your organization a common selling language and communication approach that will support you in developing and implementing strategies to close prospect(s)s, revitalize non-performing customers, and close business that has stalled. And though it is possible that you may stumble upon this approach after years of trial and error, you may take the fast track and read this book. You'll discover that our techniques have a broad base of applicability that enable you to become highly effective in the full scope of your business and personal life. Let this book take you to the top of your game.

Special thanks to our wives Kathy Thorsvig and Signy Hayden for massive support and encouragement during four years of writing this book. To Brad Mathews, who introduced us, for his valuable input and story in the ERB chapter.

Contact: http:/Jamesbhayden.com

©Hal Thorsvig and James Hayden

Chapter 1

Introduction

How often have you ended a sales discussion or left a sales call completely satisfied that you have engaged a viable prospect(s)? Or is a more likely scenario one where you question what you could have said or done differently? Do you wonder if you should get back to the prospect(s) or wait for the prospect(s) to get back to you? Did you feel as though you left a good impression? Did you handle the prospect's questions appropriately? When I pose these questions to salespeople, the expressions on their faces indicate that, "Yes, this happens to me." And as they look around, they see from the expressions on the faces of their colleagues that they are not alone.

We don't want salespeople to be left questioning the impact of their initial sales contacts. We certainly don't want a sense of confusion to linger in the mind of the salesperson. The bigger question that needs answering is, "How can I, as a salesperson, conduct an initial sales call feeling totally satisfied that this contact will most likely produce the business I'm hoping to obtain?"

The simple answer is control. However, who is or who should be in control? The salesperson? No question, the salesperson manages control of the selling process, and my objective is to teach you, the salesperson, to control the selling process to become the stellar salesperson you know you can be.

Managing control of the process and managing to stay in front of the prospects requires an understanding of the communication that occurs during the sales call.

What does controlling the selling process have to do with communication? Do we try to out talk? Do we wait for a pause in the conversation so that we can quickly jump in with our presentation? Do we merely defer to the prospects and allow them to direct the conversation?

Therapists have long suggested that every form of human communication involves a search for control by both or all parties. And this desire for control begins early in life. It can be subtle or not so subtle. Picture, for example, a mother trying to talk a two-year-old into eating a meal instead of playing. The adult decides it is lunchtime. The child continues to play. Food enticements are introduced. The child shows no interest. More play time after lunch is dangled as a reward. Still, no response from the toddler. So, with a swift motion, the mother scoops up the child and plops him at the lunch spot. It took some patience and subtlety, but the objective is met, and the parent maintains control. An experienced parent understands the toddler's need for control and understands the responsibilities of the parent. A less-experienced parent may end up exasperated and with an unhappy toddler if, during the exchange, the child is allowed to control the situation.

Though we are not comparing a toddler to a prospect or a salesperson to an exasperated parent, this example illustrates how early in life our search for control is introduced.

Like the experienced parent, the stellar salesperson knows how to manage or control the specific selling situation. A less-experienced salesperson is more likely to let control go to the prospect. How does this happen? I developed a diagram to help you understand exactly what occurs when a prospect controls the selling situation. I label this diagram the Universal Buying Process because it describes what will ALWAYS occur when a prospect controls the selling situation.

The diagram below illustrates the starting point for the 1st step in the process, the greeting or rapport step where both parties are on the same track.

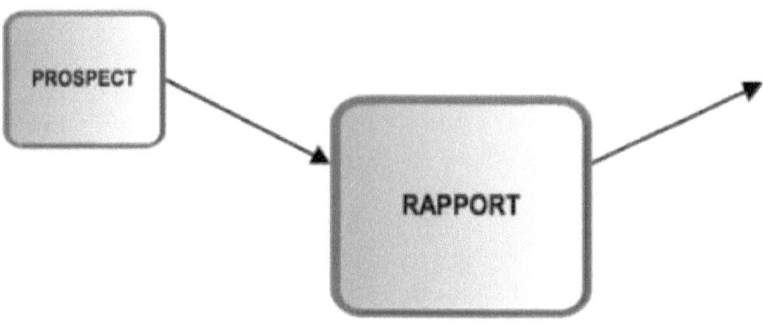

RAPPORT

The prospect(s) and salesperson both use the greeting as a rapport building stage. Each works to make a connection. Conversational chitchat develops a common ground for questions and answers. But when the salesperson asks about problems, the prospect denies any. What has happened? Didn't the salesperson establish rapport? Doesn't the prospect want to solve a problem?

Check the diagram and you see that the prospect advances to the 1st step of the Universal Buying Process, denial.

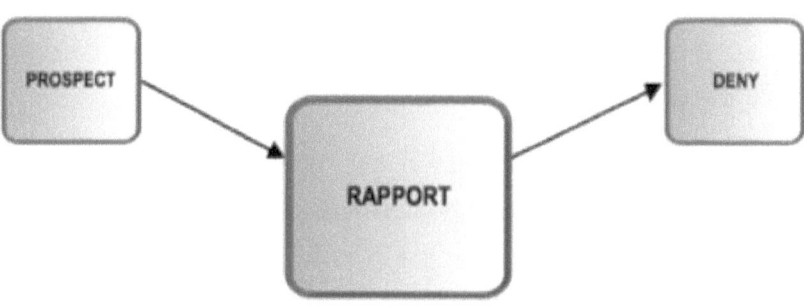

PROSPECT DENIAL

Let's take a step back. The prospect has just denied any problems within the company, and the salesperson is stuck wondering what it is he's doing here again. There are several reasons for prospect's denial. A prospect risks exposing a vulnerable area within the company if an issue is revealed. Perhaps he, himself, feels vulnerable. Prospects may also see salespeople as slick, dishonest, and perhaps liars. Not a positive image for the salesperson. But it is likely a salesperson who fits one of these descriptors has done business with he prospects, making the prospects now wary of all salespeople.

There are many examples of prospect's denial of a problem. The following narrative illustrates one.

A well-known Japanese company had rolled out a new product in Japan and had announced a rollout of the same product in the U.S. within the next six months. It was just at this time that our technology consulting company had an initial meeting scheduled with them. We had information that calls and emails to customer service in Japan had brought down the customer service system or CRM system in Japan, creating widespread customer dissatisfaction. If we could sell them our CRM solution for the U.S. market, they would have satisfied customers and be able to support a large sales volume. This was a great opportunity for our company. I contacted the prospects to discuss our CRM solution for U.S. customer support. The prospects immediately denied there was a problem, claiming there was no support issue and that their company was more than ready to roll out the new product in the U.S. Conversation over!

Why did the prospects deny the existence of the customer support problem? What motivates prospects to deny obvious or exposed problems? It is a deeper desire to conceal or shield the company's or the prospect's true circumstances. Why does this happen? We as individuals tend to make decisions according to our own best interests. the prospects intend to control what is best for them and/or their company. From' the prospects perspective it is not in their best interest to reveal a problem that exposes an area of vulnerability within the business. Vulnerability implies weakness and the opportunity to be taken advantage of by a salesperson. A person in control cannot be weak.

Did the Japanese prospects decide according to their or the company's best interests? Yes, if you understand the company's wish to not appear lacking, regarding control of the customer support system. They chose to deny a problem existed even when evidence pointed to the contrary. Prospect denial gives control to the prospect, allowing the prospect to feel less vulnerable.

Now what? Does the sales call end here? Possibly, but you may find the prospect continues to express interest in the salesperson's product or service as part of the attempt to maintain control in the sales call.

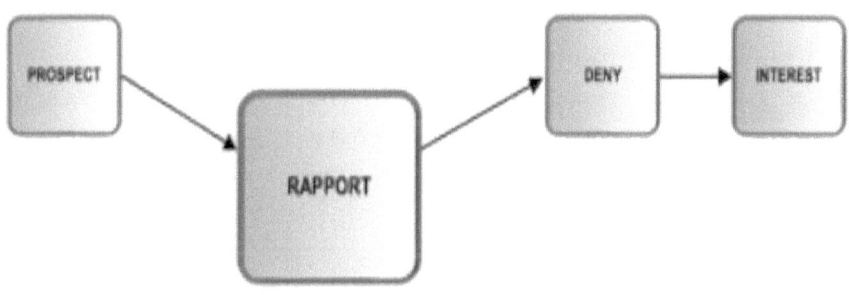

PRODUCT INTEREST

Questions from the prospect are a good sign to the salesperson.

The prospects may be truly INTERESTED and truly in need of your solution. Your solutions are a fit for their company. So, to SATISFY INTEREST in your product, you provide them with your features and benefits presentation. You even offer up a price quote and ARMED with enough information about your solution, are now able to compare you with your competitors and perhaps strike a deal with them. And all of this, They the prospects were able to do for free because you offered up a solution. Product information comes with a price for both you and the prospect. The cost to you and steep the cost to them.

Here is a lesson in an unqualified product presentation. It is a reminder of the cost to the salesperson of an unqualified presentation.

I sold incentive programs early in my career to technology companies. The programs were developed to entice the distribution channels to buy one company's product over another company's. I was working with a major player in the industry at the time and calling on them several times a week to set up an initial meeting. I received a call from the company telling me they were ready for an incentive program, and I should come in to make a presentation.

I met with the CMO and other executives. I ran through our capabilities, took their questions, and heard their compliments on our company's experience and my presentation. One of the executives asked, "What differentiates your company from the competition? What's your secret sauce? How do you do it? What would you design for us, tell us, and that will help us to make a favorable decision?"

Excited for the opportunity to close as my first sale such an important one, I proceeded to the whiteboard and presented our solution. We agreed to touch base the following week, and two weeks passed before I was able to reach someone at the company, and this is what I heard.

"Oh, yeah. I've been meaning to call you. We like you and your company. But we are some of the smartest people here in the world. Your programs are not rocket science, and now we can do this on our own, so we are moving forward with our own incentive program. Thanks for everything. Have a nice day!"

Not the conversation I expected to have, but it was a lesson well learned. Do not ever present product information to an unqualified prospect!

ENTHUSIASM

Why do salespeople continue tossing their pitches to the prospect? The prospect throw out compliments to them on their superior product and PRODUCT knowledge. The price quote is fabulous. The prospects implies future business is in the works. What a great salesperson you are. And who doesn't enjoy a compliment! It is easy to become caught up in this moment of mutual enthusiasm. It seems like the perfect sale, yet do you have the sale? Think of the number of times you have bought lunch, dinner, drinks for a prospect, discussed company business, worked to develop a good business relationship, and still not seen business materialize. The following story illustrates an experience I had relying on my rapport building skills to solidify a business deal.

Once again, early in my career, I met a young executive, around my age, working with a large forest products' company, who assured me my product was a perfect fit for his company and we should work well together. We went out for at least twenty meals and perhaps ten sporting events over a period of a couple of years. It seemed that we were always just on the cusp of business. But at the end of that time, still no business.

I was basing my business relationship with him on what I thought was his enthusiasm for my product and my ability to work with him and his company. Instead of being a true business relationship, the individual used me to acquire our product knowledge and enjoy the free meals and baseball tickets.

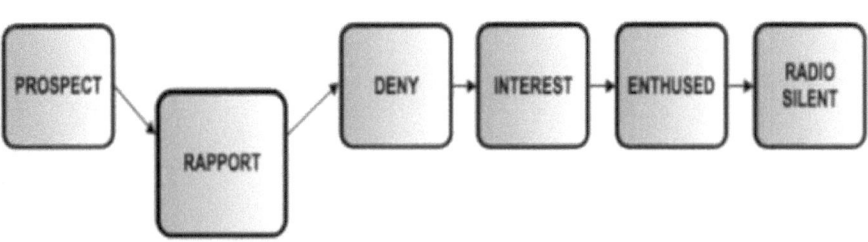

RADIO SILENT

For me as for most salespeople, it takes time to process what happens next. It is usually an elated salesperson who waits for the order to come in, still thinking a sale is imminent. However, phone calls to the prospects are not returned, and emails go unanswered. What the salesperson sees as future business in the pipeline is in fact inaccurate. When a prospect goes "radio silent," the salesperson has less than a 10% chance of sales success. Most people don't like to say no. It is easier to ignore requests for a return email text, or phone call. It is the unqualified buyer's default to go Radio Silent.

We have all been here. In my 30 years of selling and working with salespeople, I have determined there is not a salesperson working, including myself, who has not been caught up in the prospect's method of control. Remember, in every communication the prospect process, each party searches for control. In a selling situation, it is the prospect's goal to control the sales process. If salespeople do not develop their own method to maintain control, they will always fall victim to the prospect's Universal Buying Process.

To combat this situation and give the salesperson a framework for staying on track, I define six factors that greatly influence the outcome of sales calls. Understanding and successfully employing these factors will help to guarantee your success in maintaining control of the selling process. These six factors include:

Timing of the Greeting

Moment of Choice Question

Emotional Reasons for Buying

Buying Influencers

Prospect's Financial Resources

Solutions

A powerful salesperson controls the sales process...not. the prospects.

THE SALESPERSON

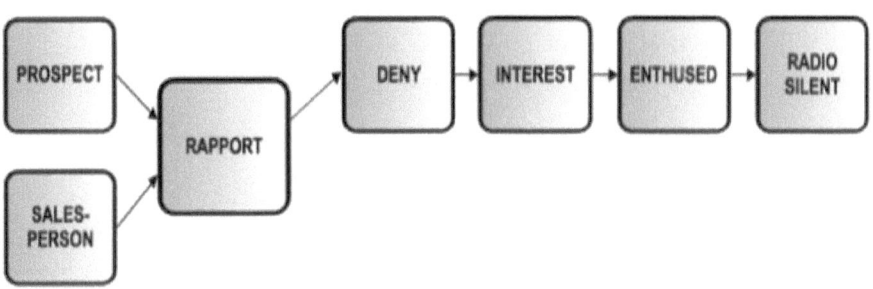

GREETING

Where does every sale begin? With the greeting and building a connection. An observant salesperson will connect with the prospect using simple clues gleaned from the office setting online, and the prospect's attire, as well as the communications to data gathered through the CRM, website, or other touches. What do you know about the prospect from their Linked in profile, other social media, and touchpoint with your company? When you are in the office are there trophies on the wall, awards, family photos? Is the prospect dressed formally or casually? Small talk addressing any of these interests or lifestyle clues is intended to develop mutual trust and interest in a very short time.

Salespeople today are selling in a global market or in a multitude of regional markets and all come with their own bonding rituals. While living and working in Texas, I could practically spend a day with discussions of bass fishing or hunting. In New York City and the major metropolitan East Coast areas, time spent on an introduction is more apt to be shortened to a nanosecond. Though obviously an exaggeration, my experience tells us that East Coast businesspeople are more eager to get down to business. And while it is imperative that regional differences are noted, the salesperson must take the initiative in keeping the greeting period to no longer than 10 to 15 minutes.

Spending more time than this indicates "call reluctance." Salespeople who face call reluctance fear hearing a prospect's "NO". Sales professionals understand this as an opportunity to find prospects who will do business with them. What is critical here? TIME. By setting a limit on rapport building, the salesperson does not allow the prospect to steal time, which in the end translates into money.

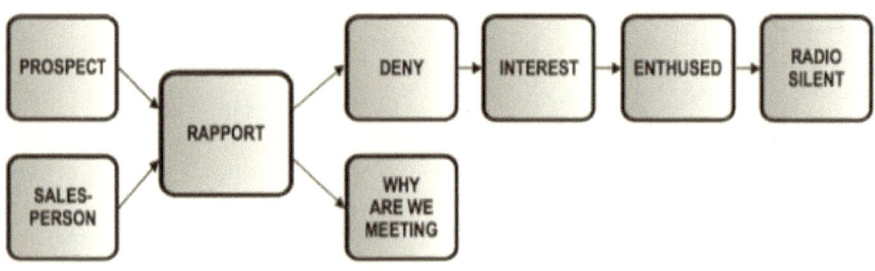

THE MOMENT OF CHOICE QUESTION

After taking a mental check on the time spent building rapport, the salesperson poses the question; "When you looked at your calendar and saw we are meeting today, why did you choose to set our meeting?" This is not usually what the prospect expects to hear, and now instead of asking the salesperson "What have you got?" the prospect is given the opportunity to reflect on issues facing him or the company. It is safe to give specific information about the company's problems or needs instead of jumping behind a smoke screen of denial. Here, a salesperson is interested in fixing something specific as opposed to selling a one-size-fits-all program or product.

In traditional selling models, the salesperson is told to build rapport; offer up some features and benefits to create interest, and then close. By asking) why they chose to meet, the salesperson will get an idea of the problems facing them. It is also an opportunity to move forward. And more importantly it is the Moment of Choice for the salesperson who intend to take control of the selling process.

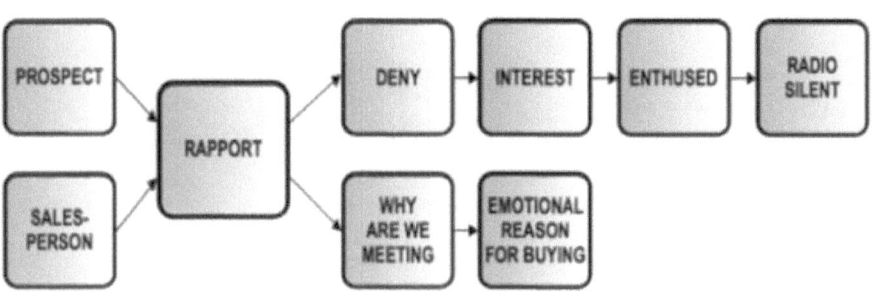

EMOTIONAL REASONS FOR BUYING (ERB)

The prospect's answer to the previous question may reveal one or more concerns. But the salesperson must dig deeper to determine the ERB or Emotional Reason for Buying. Why? Emotions tend to rule our buying behavior. Two emotions linked to buying behavior are pleasure and pain. It is easy to see this rule applied to the casual shopper who will often buy for pleasure, but in a business setting, ERB is the more intense emotion that drives prospects to buy. An awareness of this ERB forces them to act now!

Those solutions/services' needs must be defined by the prospects emotional attachment to those needs. In other words, the salesperson must help the prospects recognize that the ERB they are experiencing can be resolved by the salesperson's product/service. For now, understand that it is essential to identify. The "stellar" salesperson will gather enough information from the prospects to detect the real ERB and produce a product or solution for the ERB.

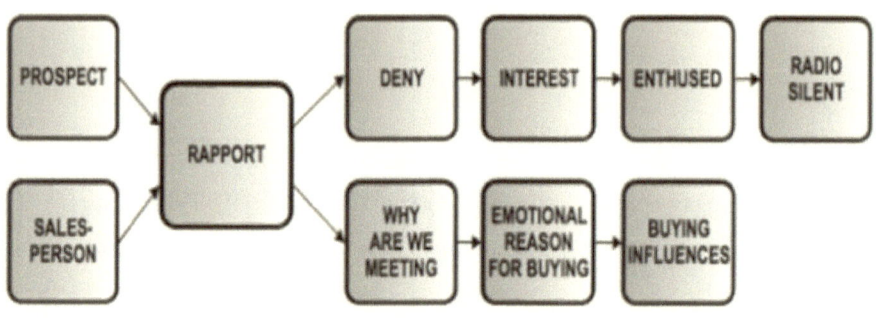

BUYING INFLUENCES

Reaching the person with the authority to approve the order can be a difficult process for many salespeople. Can the prospect say "yes"? Can they say "no" when everyone else has said "yes"? Do they have signing authority? For years I have worked with salespeople who spend considerable time presenting products or services that were well received only to discover that the prospects could not make the buying decision. I teach the salesperson to identify the various buying influencers within the company. Understand them and you will reach the person with the signing authority!

I was selling incentives to boost market share and sales of semiconductor companies. The well-known company I approached saw its market share and sales chewed up by a competitor offering similar incentives to its distributors. My contact assured me that he oversaw marketing and had responsibility and budget for my company's incentive program. It was as good as sold, according to the prospect. He was careful to control all my contacts in the organization. I had not met with the executive team, and was assured that that wasn't needed, even though I insisted. The contact merely needed a sign off from the executive team, who was in favor of our incentives, and it was a done deal. The business case yielded a 256 to 1 ROI, a no-brainer, and he said he had the executive team in his pocket on this one.

Several anxious days passed with no word from my passionate prospective customer. Finally, a text to call ASAP. "Ahhh, some unanticipated news. Your program was killed by the CFO. Seems we need a new parking lot, and the fixed costs must go there. Sorry, we'll try again next year."

Clearly, I did not research the Buying Influencers and let the prospect control the buying process.

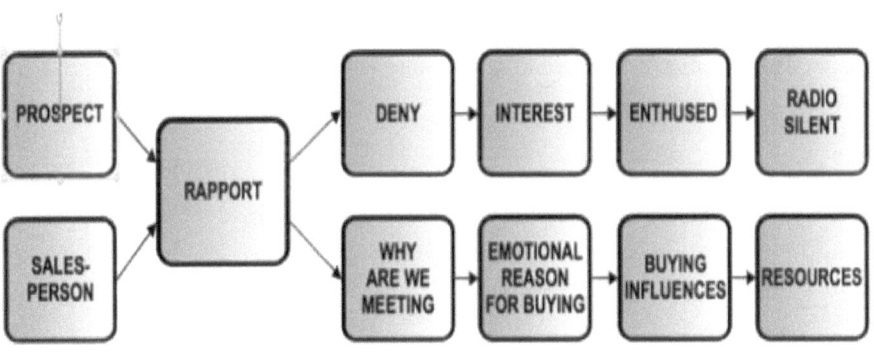

RESOURCES

Money issues in the selling process are reported by salespeople to be one of the most difficult areas to resolve. Why do we find ourselves backing away from talk about money? Could it be the social taboo that we just don't talk about money? Could it be the salespersons fear that if money comes up too early in the selling process, the prospect will back away? I think it is some of both. Our social mores restrict us from discussing personal money. Who asks their neighbors how much they make? We typically do not have conversations about our income or others' incomes.

In business dealings, it is the salespersons' job to confirm the resources are available, and only then are they able to move to the next step.

SOLUTION

When the prospects is qualified, the salesperson moves to the product or services that are available, or in other words, the Solution. At this point in the sales call, the salesperson has already confirmed the reason for being there, uncovered the pain, discovered the buying influencers, and determined the resources. Now is the opportunity for the salesperson to produce the sales solutions material and define the benefits of the products or services offered. How different is this sequence from the one in which the prospect control the sale and acquires product knowledge in the initial stage of the selling process?

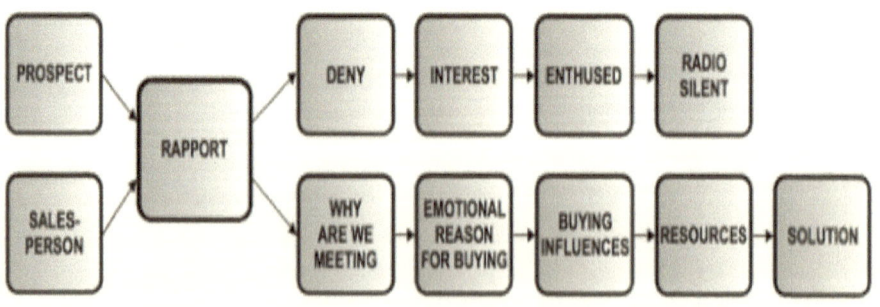

CONFIRMATION

The prospect wants the solution and agrees to purchase the product or service. The salesperson confirms the order and compliments the prospect's smart decision in making the purchase. Is the sale closed? NO! The salesperson can only consider the deal closed when the payment is received. We will learn in Chapter 9 a three-step Prospect confirmation process.

We have outlined the various stages of successful selling, and in the following chapters we'll devote more time to each aspect of these stages of the selling process. The success or failure of a sale is often determined by the ability of the salesperson to control the sale. The choice is yours. Will you control the selling process or allow the prospect to control you?

Take a moment to review the diagram. Your "Moment of Choice" occurs in the initial stage of the selling process. You set the time limit for introductions and initiate the process with the first question. If you stay on track, you'll stay in control of the selling process. You'll gain the respect of the prospect by empowering them to make the decision to solve their problems with your product or service.

Chapter Highlights

Chapter 1 Introduction

Need for control with the prospect(s) and salesperson.

Prospect(s)

- Rapport

- Prospect(s) denial: denying a problem exists.

- Product Interest: presenting too early.

- Enthusiasm: looks good

Salesperson

- Timing of greeting: limit time on rapport building.

- Moment of choice question: why did you choose to meet?

- Emotional reasons for buying- pleasure and pain. Both are the emotional reasons for buying.

- Buying Influencers: have you identified and met with all buying influencers?

- Financial resources: have confirmation that resources are available.

- Solutions: discuss product or service/solution.

- Confirmation: reconfirm the order.

Chapter 2

Dynamic Positioning Statement

I was responsible for West Coast revenue for loyalty programs directed to companies interested in frequent flier and frequent buyer campaigns. I had, finally, arranged a meeting with one of the big hotel companies wishing to put in place a frequent guest campaign. When the entire executive team including the chairman attended, I thought "WOW, all the decision makers are here they must be very interested." Deciding they had done their investigative homework on our company, I was determined not to disappoint them. The inexperienced team I brought with me was eager to answer questions that arose. How do we track the company's performance? What do we name it? How do we communicate it? What is a ballpark estimate of our fees? What are our formulas? Can you show us your samples? Excited at the prospect of a big sale, we eagerly proceeded to fill in all the blanks. We were going to sell our first major loyalty program.

The team and I left the meeting high fiving each other. Only after the excitement of the meeting had died down did I realize I didn't know their budget or if they were buying. I had neglected to ask about competitors. After weeks of trying to get in touch with the company, I contacted the VP of Marketing who, after an awkward silence, told me that though our programs were great, they felt they could build the loyalty program themselves and save about $1.5 million. I lost control and spilled the GOLD again, and therefore lost an important and lucrative sale.

Haven't we all heard the adage worth its weight in GOLD?

From earliest times GOLD emerged as a commodity coveted and valued by individuals and nations. Its rarity and beauty created a desirability and fascination for all things GOLD, and so GOLD took on a power, giving it a place in history unlike any other commodity. Nations based economies on the GOLD standard. Ancient peoples identified GOLD with strength, power, and immortality. Consider the amount of GOLD found in tombs of the Egyptians. GOLD inspired legends and continues to be the medium used by jewelers to create our most precious and unique ornaments.

Though the GOLD standard is no longer the basis for our currency, it continues to function as the principal financial asset of many foreign currencies and governments and is held by central banks as a way of hedging against loans to their own governments as "internal reserve." GOLD coins and bars widely traded in today's market still serve as a private store of wealth for individuals. GOLD in our lives today continues to be a constant source of inspiration, valued and desired for its rarity.

You as a salesperson bring solutions to the marketplace as quantifiable as GOLD. Your solutions can impart power to businesses, allowing the business to increase sales, improve production, encourage creativity, and sustain market share. Businesses buying your solutions could stand above the rest and be envied for their successes in an ever-changing marketplace landscape. The salesperson becomes the player with the power when one considers the solution akin to GOLD, because your solution to marketplace issues can make or break many a business. Your GOLD is the desired commodity in a sales call. If the salesperson can see themselves as the medium controlling the potential wealth of the prospect(s), then that person will control the sales call as well.

As the player with the power, consider how you would like to manage your GOLD. Does it make sense to offer it all up immediately? Do you think the prospect(s) recognizes its value? Can the prospect(s) offer you reasonable terms for your GOLD? Does the prospect(s) even have a use for it?

Unfortunately, most salespeople fail to recognize the importance of the role they play in this scenario. When I ask salespeople, "Does your product or service bring considerable or even great value to the marketplace?" the response is invariably an emphatic, "Yes!" As a follow up, I ask, "Can your product or service solve the problems your prospects are experiencing?" Again, they answer affirmatively. Finally, I ask, "Do you have any prospects who want your services/products without having to compensate you for it?" A predictably sheepish smile creeps over the faces of the salespeople. You can imagine their collective answers as they say, "Of course!"

What has happened here? The prospects have indicated a need for the marketplace solutions, acknowledged its value, and yet seem merely to be stringing you along. Is that their goal? Perhaps. Do they believe they can procure something for nothing? Possibly. Are you willing to unload all your GOLD early with a detailed explanation of your product/service, that is, offer them your solution to their problem for nothing in return? Most definitely not! How then, does the salesperson offer up a small nugget of GOLD to stay in the game without giving the game away?

Let's look at the Dynamic Positioning Statement or DPS.

Too often a salesperson will eagerly respond to the prospect's question, "What can you tell me about your product/service?" with a highly detailed explanation of the product/service offered. Isn't this just the opener the salesperson is waiting to hear? Now he can make his feature and benefit dump. After all, a competent salesperson will have a tremendous investment in product knowledge and benefits and will bring his enthusiasm for the product/service to the sales call and be all too happy to share this information with the prospect, imagining the perfect sale.

How can the salesperson prepare for this inevitable question? How much information should he/she provide? Is company history important? Is product information, sales testimonials, and name-dropping effective? Does the question need an answer?

Enter the Dynamic Positioning Statement or DPS. This is THE answer to the prospect's question for your company information. At the same time, it opens the window of opportunity for a question-and-answer process with the prospect that leads to qualifying or perhaps disqualifying that prospect.

What is DPS? It is a statement that clearly defines the types of customers you work with, what solutions are available for your customers through your product/service, and a specific, third-party report about the results your customers experience because of using your product/service. A DPS will tell the prospect(s) WHO are your customers, WHAT you do for your customers, and WHAT are the RESULTS your customers report because of using your product or service.

A DPS example: We work with business owners and executives, sales managers, and salespeople to support them build their selling skills. Our clients report, because of our program, sales increase up to 50%. Tell me about your company and what you do.

What is the REAL importance of the DPS? With a DPS in place, the salesperson avoids falling into the trap of an early, informal presentation of product/service benefits. With this statement, we have not told the prospect HOW we do something, simply what we do. Telling the HOW of the product/service is the beginning of giving away the GOLD.

With a DPS, the salesperson's company is differentiated their from businesses using a formula statement to sell product/service benefits to the masses. How does the salesperson go about developing the DPS? Let's step back and look at the three basic elements of the statement:

WHO your customers are.

WHAT you do for your customers

What RESULTS your customers experience when using your product/service?

Another benefit of a clearly rehearsed and succinct DPS is a link to the pulse of the marketplace. How does this fit with a DPS?

The marketplace is never static. Take for example a salesperson selling a product/service for more than ten years. Is that product/service the same today as it was ten years ago? Not likely. Is that person's DPS the same today as it was ten years ago? Again, not likely. When did the need to re-think their DPS get noticed? Probably when the information in the DPS no longer elicited interest from the prospect(s), or worse, became inaccurate in the sales call.

The marketplace is dynamic and ever-changing. Products and services become obsolete at the fastest pace in history, just as the horse and buggy went out of favor after the invention of the automobile. A cell phone today cannot compare to the cell phone of even a few years ago. Think of the DPS as an early warning system to alert us to subtle and sometimes not so subtle changes in the marketplace. Develop a Dynamic Positioning Statement and continue to revise it dependent upon its relevance in your marketplace.

In the late 90's I was involved in working with business and technology executives with a solution that sorted out how to utilize the websites social media to maximize their business and make more money. Over 90% of my clients asked us back for more work within a year.

Today there are tools that anyone can utilize to have a website presence, and drive internet traffic, and websites can be built and operated in the hundreds of dollars per year rather than hundreds of thousands as it was eleven years ago.

What happened?

Social and digital media was non-existent then, and now it is the fastest growing media available.

Blackberry™ were new devices, yet most people now would not consider looking at video or an ad on a Blackberry™. The bandwidth of wireless connection speed was slow, and the screens were poor.

Thirteen-year-olds are now able to develop websites, and there is a lot more to communicating on the Internet and text now with the proliferation of social media and mobile apps and websites.

Did you know in June 2011, it was reported that there is more communication through mobile apps than the Internet? Being an Internet expert, being an expert about mobile phones is key. And today it is AI.

My statement today:

I work with top brands and advertising executives to develop and implement mobile advertising. My clients report they make money than they expected with the mobile applications because of our service.

A caveat: when selling highly complicated or technical products, eliminate buzzwords and technical jargon and terms that are typically understood by only a small segment of a company or industry. It is only confusing and possibly intimidating. A good adage when developing the DPS is to ask yourself how would I articulate my product/service to a seven-year-old child? It is surprising what clarity is brought to the picture when one is forced to tell a story in its simplest terms.

Chapter Highlights

Chapter 2 Dynamic Positioning Statement (DPS)

- Create a statement that defines:

- Types of customers you work with.

- Solutions available through your product/service.

- Third-party experience/results with your product or service.

- Avoid telling how or a presentation. It spills the GOLD at this juncture.

Chapter 3

MEETING AGENDA

In 1863, Henry Martyn Robert, a military engineer, was asked to chair a church meeting. Not pleased with his ability to lead the meeting, Robert decided to learn how to run a meeting and studied parliamentary procedures before developing a rulebook titled Pocket Manual of Rules of Order for Deliberate Assemblies, that we know today as Robert's Rules of Order. How does this book connect with salespeople and selling? The author concluded that a successful business meeting should have an agenda that includes the order in which things occur, the subject matter, the time allotted for the meeting, and an initial agreement by the majority on changes that take place in the meeting. A sales call is a business meeting and therefore needs an agenda. This meeting agenda is an oral or written agreement between the prospect(s) and the salesperson and will contain four parts.

- Agreement on the desired outcome of the meeting for the prospect(s) and review of the time allocated to accomplish the desired outcome.

- Agreement for each party to share information relevant to the meeting.

- Agreement with the prospect(s) to decline your offer.

- Agreement for ongoing communications between all pertinent Buying Influences and the salesperson.

We'll take a closer look at each of the four agenda parts of a sales call in the next few pages.

TIME and Outcome – STEP I

Rapport-building skills are a must for a salesperson, and even the most skilled can become caught up in the conversation while engaging a prospect. With good conversation, time flies, and when the prospect checks his watch to say time is up for him, the salesperson realizes too late that no business took place. The salesperson must establish before the meeting how much time the prospect will give to the business meeting. Giving the prospect the opportunity to set the meeting time allotment indicates a consideration for the time constraints we all face. The hours of the workday are equally distributed, and respecting the prospect's time is a valuable rapport-building component. In addition, it gives the salesperson a clear understanding of the time in which he must understand the prospect's problem. An effective "time" question is as simple as, "Thanks for agreeing to meet today. Do we have a hard stop or a set time to stop our meeting?"

With the time allotment agreed upon, next is an agreement on an outcome. In a stereotypical sales call, the features and benefits dump to create interest follows rapport building. This monologue by the salesperson is the hit or miss attempt to identify the prospect's true buying motives. Our method teaches the salesperson to focus on the prospect's needs with questions that will identify buying motives. And the first question deals with the outcome of the current meeting. "In our meeting today, if YOU had a perfect outcome, what would it be we have covered when it comes to my product or service?"

Where is the focus? The prospects at the outset we focus on the prospect and what is important to them. Why do we do this? It allows you, the salesperson, to eliminate the guesswork by simply focusing the prospect on, needs, which is after all the reason you are here. The salesperson is here to get an understanding of the problem, because without knowledge of the problem the salesperson cannot be effective.

QUESTION – STEP II

The second step in the Meeting Agenda is to establish an agreement for each party to share information. The temptation is great for the typical salesperson to do a product demo or product pitch once the foot is in the door. However, this style runs counter to our data and teachings. Skillful communication is still a valuable tool for the salesperson, but instead of taking the stage with product information, the salesperson communicates using a question-and-answer technique. The prospect typically waits for the product info, but we want to change this way of thinking This may best be accomplished by getting an agreement that both parties share information. An agreement for both parties to share information provides the salesperson with valuable information about the company while at the same time allowing the prospect to identify the problem(s) for themselves.

REMOVE THE PRESSURE – STEP III

There is probably nothing worse than feeling as though you are being boxed into a corner, and that feeling is common among prospects, who agree to meet with a salesperson and then realize they don't want to be "sold." Perhaps the prospects have second thoughts about buying or simply want to hear what is new in the market and is now just trying to figure out how to say 'no thanks' to the salesperson. To avoid this situation, we introduce step three in the oral agenda: remove the pressure. We offer the prospects the opportunity to decline the offer. An example of this would be: "If you believe that you are not going to go forward with this, are you ok telling me no?" If the prospect discovers our offer is the solution, the salesperson must learn what kind of process the prospects will go through to buy the solution.

Why would a salesperson, at the beginning of the call, want to give the prospect an out? What is the advantage to the salesperson? Feeling boxed in puts the individual in a defensive position. Picture the prospect with hands up, warding off any further conversation. Is the prospect in a comfortable spot? Probably not. Is there the likelihood the salesperson can have any meaningful communication that will advance the sale? Probably not. But we can move him from defensive to comfortable by allowing them the opportunity to decline the offer. In doing this, the salesperson assures the prospect(s) that are is not there to "'take them to the mat."

ONGOING COMMUNICATION & BUYING INFLUENCERS Step IV

Your prospects are moving closer to becoming clients, and Step IV in the meeting agenda will position them for becoming clients. At this point the salesperson and prospects agree to ongoing communication to follow this initial meeting. Without the agreement to follow up with text, email, direct message or voice mail, the prospects could easily fall into "radio silent mode." And no salesperson wants to find themselves waiting to see if a deal is still alive. A clear statement dealing with open future communication between the salesperson and all buying influencers is another essential ingredient to the four-step meeting agenda.

Early in my sales career, I was involved in enterprise-marketing solutions. A relatively new, rapidly growing company in the Seattle area had a reputation for hiring the "smartest people in the world." They were also known to have a load of cash for marketing solutions. After six months of prospecting, I finally scored a meeting with the VP responsible for the marketing budgets. I didn't need to qualify her, as I heard from colleagues that she was the "one." I was sure she would see a need for the services I had to sell to her. Her only response was by email, which meant no phone contact with her prior to our meeting. And I was so delighted to have a meeting scheduled after months of asking for a meeting that I neglected to ask my typical questions of the Big Prospect.

* What marketing plans did she have for the next year?

* What are the big issues she was facing?

*Who else is involved in these types of initiatives and do they need to be included in the meeting?

*Why is she interested in meeting with me?

* What does success look like in our meeting?

* If it is a successful meeting, what will happen next?

I knew these questions were necessary for a successful first meeting and for the Big Prospect; I threw these questions out the window because our CEO was calling me every week about getting a meeting with this company. And hearing that I had the meeting, he let out 128 decibel Whoop!

Every ounce of my being was crying out to be the star of the company—to be loved, to be the man. Every insecurity in my life came up: why did my birthparents give me up, why was I picked on in Junior High, why didn't girls like me until I was well into high school? I was lucky as hell to be meeting with this woman; really, why should she meet with me anyway? Would she see me as the late-blooming, gawky nerd that was looking for love and validation through this meeting?

Wow! I felt I was lucky just to go to a meeting with her at this premier company. And I needed to add another big sale to the quarter to support my daughter's private school tuition and the new vacation home I acquired. This call will be fine; I am persuasive, and I will wing it. She will buy.

The big day arrived, she confirmed by text a half-hour meeting, and I was certain that she would be so enthralled by our product that she would meet with me for much longer. I was nervous on the drive to the company's suburban campus and was awed by the fact that she may be smarter than I am. When I checked in at the lobby and signed in on the computer, I was so shaky that I had a difficult time seeing the computer screen. Since I was early, I had time to run through the meeting in my head. After what seemed like quite a lengthy wait, the Big Prospect came through the door. I shook hands hoping she wouldn't notice how sweaty my palms were.

My nervousness showed through when I tried to win her over with my personal bonding questions. "Are you from Seattle? Cleveland, great — didn't a river catch fire there, or was that Detroit? So, how do you like the weather in Seattle? Yeah, that's why I have lived here most of my life." Thinking I was a dead man walking and hoping to turn this around, I noticed she had on a ring and asked, "Do you have children? Oh, you and your partner have decided not to have kids."

Now I felt as though I was walking to the execution chamber and wondered if I would have a last meal when she offered me a soda or coffee. I went for the water since my throat was so dry. Once in her office she reached behind the computer screen, grabbed a cooking timer, tick, tick, tick. She stated that I had 30 minutes and said she had a "hard stop." This was my first exposure to the term hard stop, and I thought, OK, I must tell her everything I know in 30 minutes. I proceeded to do just that. I could see how interested she was with the questions she asked, and if I tell her everything, she will see how smart I am and then naturally buy from me.

The timer sounded, and she asked if I would send a soft copy of my presentation with our recommendations. When I returned to the office to call our CEO, doubt began to settle in. "Why would she buy? Does she have a budget? Is she able to buy? Why didn't I ask those questions?" But I promised to send out our recommendations so, pushing off a meeting with my biggest current client; I followed up with the document. For the next two months, I attempted to contact the Big Prospect until one day I heard through the grapevine that the company was rolling out a campaign just like the one we discussed in our meeting with a competitor. My ideas, even the name of the campaign, was very close to my recommendations.

After several weeks, I received an email from the Big Prospect saying the company had decided to go with another company. This is outrageous, I thought. How can they execute their campaign with our company's ideas? Isn't that illegal? Or was I dumb? How had I lost control of the sale? I realized I had not followed the sales process that we are advocating in this book. Like a losing sports team, I got away from my game plan, played by someone else's rules, and wasted a lot of time and money.

Here is the agenda from a pivotal sales meeting with the same company two years later that ultimately netted $2,000,000 in sales for our company.

Agenda:

- Allocate time for the meeting.

- Establish an ideal outcome.

The salesperson must establish before the meeting how much time the prospect(s) will give to the business meeting. Giving the prospect(s) the opportunity to set the meeting time allotment indicates a consideration for the time constraints we all face.

The next question deals with the outcome of the current meeting. "In our meeting today, if YOU had a perfect outcome, what would we have covered when it comes to my product or service?"

- Share information.

Establish an agreement for each party to share information. The temptation is great for the typical salesperson to do a product demo or product presentation once the foot is in the door. However, this style runs counter to our data and teachings. Skillful communication is still a valuable tool for the salesperson, but instead of taking the stage with product information, the salesperson communicates using a question-and-answer technique.

- Say no or move forward.

Offer the prospects the opportunity to decline the offer. If they discover our offer is the solution, the salesperson must learn what kind of process the prospects will go through to buy the solution.

- If a good outcome

- Define and introduce to others involved.

- Return text, direct messages, e-mail, and phone calls.

- Say no at any time or discuss roadblocks.

At this point the salesperson and prospects agree to ongoing communication to follow this initial meeting. Without the agreement to follow up with text, direct messages, email or voice mail, the prospect could easily fall into radio silent mode.

- Establish method for ongoing communications.

The party that controls the agenda will likely control the outcome of the meeting. I would encourage all salespeople to write their own meeting agenda in words that best fit their speech patterns and develop a standard format for a written meeting agenda. Put a copy next to the telephone. Carry it on a sales call and present it to your prospects. Use it! There is magic to producing a written document, and it places the salesperson in control. My clients tell me having a well-practiced oral or written Meeting Agenda is the single most distinguishing behavior to produce early improvement that forces results in their selling process.

Chapter Highlights

Chapter 3

Meeting Agenda

Agreement between prospects and salesperson and contains:

- Agreement on time allocated for the meeting and agreement on the outcome for the prospect.

- Agreement for each party to share information.

- Agreement for the prospects to say no or move forward.

- Agreement for the prospect ongoing communication between all pertinent buying influencers and the salesperson.

Chapter 4

EMOTIONAL REASONS FOR BUYING

It goes without saying that emotions play enormous roles in our lives, from our first great loves to our greatest fears. Emotions can be controlled or uncontrolled, strong, or weak. Emotions motivate us for action or inaction. And in selling/finding buyers we look for those emotional motivators that cause the prospects to act. Both pleasure and pain motivate an individual to action, but of the two, pain is by far the stronger motivator, and we'll examine this as a motivating factor for buying in a selling situation.

I need a new car. Or rather should I say I want a new car? I can picture myself driving to my next sales call or class reunion in my new, black four door Mercedes with all the bells and whistles. I don't really need a new car. The car I drive now is quite satisfactory, is mechanically sound, and gets me where I need to go. But I would feel so good driving this car, and wouldn't it make me look that much more successful? I begin to wonder if my old car makes a statement about my success or lack of it. Am I embarrassed being seen in my car?

With the vision of seeing myself driving down the street in my new car, I head to the dealership or website. I am greeted by a salesperson or chatbot and tell them I'm thinking of getting a new car and would like to look around. And first, I start with questions about the various models. What type of engine does it have? How is the mileage? What comes with the warranty? Certainly, these questions are relevant. But is this truly the reason I came to buy a car in the first place? No. My trip to the car dealer or website started with an emotional need to look more successful. I wanted to take away the *pain* of embarrassment. And now to qualify that need to erase the pain, I ask questions based on practical reasons to purchase. I would look rather silly asking the salesperson or chatbot, how do I look in the car, but that question more accurately reflects the reason I am at the dealership or website in the first place.

The purpose of this story is to illustrate our reasons for buying, which are typically emotional reasons. It is embarrassing for me to appear less successful because of the older car I drive. I can relieve that embarrassment with the purchase of the car I really want to own. I can satisfy the intellectual need to purchase the new car with the questions I ask the salesperson or chatbot. So, on the strength of this ERB I buy a new car. In every sales situation, emotional reasons for buying significantly influence the sale.

Why is it that the pain of something motivates the buyer? We find that pleasurable experiences can often be delayed, and people will generally act more immediately to avoid discomfort. How many of you have found a prospect spending money purely out of pleasure upon seeing a new product? Not likely.

If pain is the motivating factor for buying, how then, do we tap into this ERB?

To convey an understanding of the concept of emotional pain, I introduce the idea of fears and pose this question in my training session. "As humans, what do you suppose is our biggest fear?" Responses vary wildly, but they are always personal and emotional and often touch on the fear of death. Does this mean we greet our next prospect with, "I know you're worried about dying, so why don't you just go ahead and tell me what your problem is?" I don't think that will quite work, and it won't exactly build trust and rapport with the prospect! and the idea here is that fear creates emotional pain. So, in a sales call, how do we identify the specific fear or fears that create the prospect's ERB?

We have all had prospects question us on our products or services. And generally, the questions are specific to their needs. These very specific questions represent an Early Warning Indicator or EWI and are used by the salesperson to determine just how emotionally the prospect engaged the prospects are with each of the underlying issues. Following is a series of questions recently asked by a prospect of a printing company.

"What is the quality of your print service?"

"What kind of technical support do you offer?"

"Are your prices competitive?"

"Is customer service readily available?"

"Do you guarantee on-time delivery?

On the surface, these questions seem straightforward. An inexperienced salesperson will answer them affirmatively and then proceed to a presentation of product information. A salesperson, using the EWI listens carefully, interpreting them quite differently. Though they all appear to be customer-related and surely can be satisfied with the salesperson's solution, the experienced salesperson sees the questions as an indication of an underlying problem (fear) facing the prospect. Many prospects have a fear of losing their jobs or a fear of not making enough money all the possible repercussions that ensue. So, we teach the salesperson to use an Early Warning Indicator or EWI.

These EWI questions present an opportunity for the salesperson to determine how emotionally engaged the prospect is with each of the underlying issues. That is, which item brought up by the prospect is causing the greatest discomfort? How do we tap into this discomfort to be able to offer a solution?

This diagram of an onion with its many layers helps to understand the process that occurs when a salesperson seeks to uncover the underlying problems causing the discomfort. As each layer of onion is peeled away, another layer of concern is revealed until the salesperson gets to the core of the problem. The five layers represent specific emotional levels that need to be reached before the real ERB can be identified.

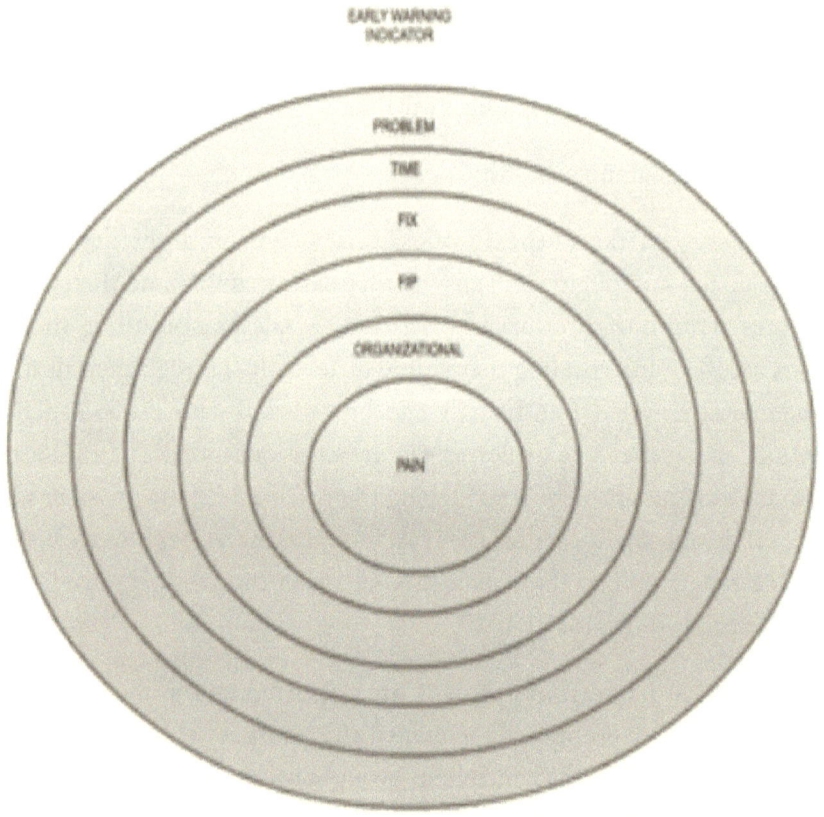

Each prospects question about a salesperson's product/service becomes an EWI trigger attached to the outer layer of the onionskin. The questions indicate a prospect's concern about a problem. It could be a concern about service, product, tech support, or any number of the prospect issues may have faced in the past or continues to face now.

We'll use our experience with the printing company prospect to support this idea as we peel away a layer at a time starting with the prospect's question, "Do you guarantee on-time delivery?"

P. "Do you guarantee on-time delivery?"

S. "And it's a problem?"

P. *Prospect has experienced a problem; 1ˢᵗ layer is peeled.*

S. "And this has been an ongoing problem?"

P. *Prospect tells duration of a problem; 2ⁿᵈ layer is peeled.*

S. "What actions have been taken to solve the shipping problem?"

P. *Prospect discusses previous solutions for a problem; 3ʳᵈ layer is peeled.*

S. "Are there any financial implications to this problem?"

P. *Financial costs to prospect are listed.*

4ᵗʰ layer "is peeled."

S. "What might compel you to fix the problem?"

P. *Prospect gives reasons to fix a problem, 5ᵗʰ layer.*

S. If the problem is solved, how will that affect your organization?"

P. *Effect of the problem on the organization and the prospect(s) personally are discovered, 6ᵗʰ layer:-*

When we view a cross section of the onion diagram, we can clearly see that it took us six questions to reach the prospect's pain. Let's analyze these six questions and note that the salesperson leads off with a comment intended to elicit more than simply a yes or no answer from the prospect. Why these questions? What sort of information do we hope to gain? How do we interpret and organize the information the answers reveal?

1ˢᵗ Question: Prospect experiences a Problem:

At the outer layer the salesperson picks an EWI trigger to confirm that a problem exists. Why? There is no reason to waste time continuing to discuss a non-existent problem, so the salesperson must choose another EWI question, if that is the case.

2ⁿᵈ Question: Duration of a Problem:

We want to know how long this problem has affected the prospect. Have delayed or late shipments been a problem for years? Months? If late shipments have persisted for years, there is a pretty good chance the prospect has learned to live with the problem. If it's a more recent issue, it's more likely that the prospect(s) will take action to fix it. Understand the duration of the problem!

3rd Question: Solutions for the Problem:

If the salesperson can determine what fixes the issue then the prospect might have already tried that did not solve the problem, the salesperson will know what not to offer. As a bonus, this question also reveals competitor information that is extremely useful.

4th Question: Financial: Financial Costs to the Prospect:

This is one of the key questions in peeling for pain. Does the prospect understand the cost of the problem? Can the prospect put into words, for example, the cost in lost sales from an under-performing salesperson?

5th Question: Reasons to Fix a Problem:

Compelling reasons to fix the problem may be related to diminished brand value, lost market share, outselling by competitors, falling behind in technology, reduced margins, increased production costs.

6th Question: Effect of the problem on the Prospect:

The salesperson has reached the core of the onion. This is the true emotional reason for buying. The salesperson listens for emotional responses from the prospect that can include words of frustration, anger, worry, fear, loss, etc.

The following narratives illustrate an understanding of the ERB concept within the context of the sales call.

A Giftware Company

The first professional sales job I had was during the early economic downturn in the 80s. I was selling / finding buyers for giftware to gift shops in Oregon and quickly realized that most of my buyers were hobbyists with slim budgets. One of the lines I represented was a collectible clown statue, and the artist had come out with his biggest collectible piece to date: a carousel that was about eight feet in circumference. It was $5000 wholesale and $10,000 retail. One of my customers, Dorothy, saw her shop as the premier place in the Northwest for clown collectors. This was her hot button. It was important for her to be seen as the Northwest leader in clown collectibles.

I had the photos of the carousel and made an appointment with Dorothy, who was operating on a small budget. I said, "Dorothy, I have a surprise for you, and before I leave today you must see something." First, I showed her some other giftware, and she bought a few things. I cautioned her to save her budget for the last item. Her largest purchase from me in the past had yet to exceed $1000. I showed her the picture of the carousel and said, "Dorothy, can you imagine having a clown collectible that no one else in the Northwest will own?" She took a deep breath and asked, "How much is it?" "$5000," I said. She recoiled.

Oh, shoot, I thought, I'm losing her, and this is the only shot I have for this big sale, but I knew her hot button was being the premier source for clown collectors. So, I suggested she come outside to the storefront and view the carousel picture in her front window. I said, "What will people say and think when they walk by your store and see the carousel in your front window? You will be seen as the Queen of Clown Collectors." Dorothy began to tear up and asked, "Where do I sign?"

Dorothy's emotional reason for buying was to be seen as having the best clown collection in the Northwest. For her, it was more important than price. So, offering her a collectible that no one else had equaled success for Dorothy. Dorothy's self-image was tied to owning the most impressive collectible clown collection, and my realizing that led to the sale.

US Truck Manufacturer

I was working with a channel sales performance programs in the mid-eighties with a national marketing group, and one of the biggest programs I had going was with a US truck manufacturer. I had a great mentor and client there, and for several years we ran an incentive reward trips for truck dealers. After the first year, my client disclosed that he used the trips to maximize attainment of his yearly personal financial objectives, which were to receive a big bonus also take a vacation to a great location with his wife. After inviting my wife and me to join them on a Caribbean cruise and poring over other possible travel destinations, I understood his personal agendas and real reason for buying our solutions. I also discovered that my client had a big financial overhead with two sons in college and he needed our programs to make his bonus and ensure he was able to help pay for his sons' educations. I helped tailor our motivational programs for the client so that he was able to achieve his bonus compensation and in effect, provide for his sons' college educations and reward himself and his wife with incredible travel destinations. Based on his success, he was promoted to senior vice president, and a part of that success was continuing with our company's performance programs.

US Luxury Car Manufacturer

I was working with a company in advertising and sponsorships on mobile applications. We were producing a mobile application for a car magazine and had been presenting to auto manufacturers. My client, one of the US luxury car manufacturers told us their company wanted to be the launch or initial sponsor of one of the mobile applications. Several weeks had gone by, and no paperwork had arrived to firm up that sale. Then a European competitor began to show an interest. I warned the US car company that this was going to sell with or without them and they needed to get the paperwork in if they wanted to be first to market. The US team stated several times that they wanted to be first to market with this new technology to show market and technological leadership. The European team sent in the order and got the app launch and sponsorship. My US client told us she would never let this happen again.

When it was decided to take a sister app to market, we called the US manufacturer first and told them this, too, would go fast. Two days later — sold!

The real reason the client bought wasn't money or budget. It was because of branding and perception. The US manufacturer didn't want a competitor to be perceived as more innovative than their company, and they found budgets to prove that. Had they failed to take advantage of the opportunity to be perceived as an innovator, the marketing executives at both the car company and the ad agency may have been fired, it was a critical time for the company. So, in effect, they bought because of a fear of being fired.

Software Company

The following story is from a former client and one of my closest friends, Brad Mathews.

I was working a major trade show where heavy construction equipment and related products were shown. Many of the show attendees were from heavy construction companies. My company provides software that, among other things, helps construction companies manage their fleet of heavy equipment more effectively. A casually dressed man walked up to me in our booth and asked to see a demonstration of our software. I replied that I would be glad to show him our software. Then I said, "There isn't something causing problems in your business that you are looking to solve?"

He said that he was having problems with allocating equipment hours and costs of his equipment to jobs. I asked if he could be more specific, and he elaborated on some of the difficulties they have in charging equipment to jobs. He also mentioned that in some cases they might not be fully billing for some of the equipment expenses that they incur.

I responded with, "It sounds like these issues can be a nagging problem for you, but they aren't costing you any real money at this point. Just to pick a number this isn't costing your business, say, $10,000 a year." He responded, "Yes, they do cost us money. In fact, the number is probably more like a half million dollars a year." Then he paused for a second and his eyes looked up and away as he redid the math in his head. "No wait, it's at least one million dollars a year."

He said this as if it were the first time, he had really put the numbers together. He seemed rather analytical about it and the dollars didn't seem to matter all that much. So, I asked him, "How do you feel about that number?" His expression changed to one of anger, he stepped forward a full step, and got right in my face saying: "Pretty god damn bad, I'm the owner of the company!" We spent the next twenty minutes reviewing specific highlights in the software that addressed these issues and agreed to schedule a full software demo in the coming days. The software purchase was concluded just a few weeks later for well over $100,000.

Chapter Highlights

Chapter 4 Emotional Reasons for Buying (ERB)*

- Pain is the motivation.

- Ask questions to find pain.

- Is there a problem?

- How long has it been a problem?

- Have they considered these fixes?

- What is the cost to the prospect?

- What is the reason to fix the problem?

- How is the prospect personally affected?

- How is the organization affected?

Chapter 5

BUYING INFLUENCERS

Have you ever made what you felt was the world's best sales presentation only to learn the people you are presenting to could not make a buying decision? Did you find yourself stalled on a deal, not able to move forward because your prospect does not make purchasing decisions? And now you don't know where to go from here. Who controls the buying decision? How do you find that information? Quite simply, you ask for it. Just how you retrieve this information is the subject of this chapter.

Sales/finding qualified buyers can be a frustrating profession, and nothing is more frustrating for salespeople than knowing they have a great product or service, are well-versed in product information, and find companies who can benefit from their product or service, yet they cannot seem to reach the individual who really can say "yes, we want your product or service!" Understanding how to ask for the decision maker is a skill that continues to elude many competent salespeople. And if you don't learn this skill, you don't move forward.

This chapter is devoted to the Buying Influencers. These are the decision makers, the players in the company who will make the decision to buy or not buy your product. It will be important to identify first the type of sale involved and then the types of individuals who have unique decision-making authority to confirm the purchase.

In my training, I describe two types of sales, the simple sale, and the complex sale. The simple sale is defined by its lower dollar volume and typically faster sale. The product or service is lower cost, and a mistake in buying the wrong service or product does not typically have far-reaching consequences. There are typically one to two decision makers. Purchasing toner cartridges is an example of a simple sale. The salesperson reaches one decision maker. If the product does not work out, the buyer returns it, or the salesperson substitutes another product or brand.

A complex sale involves a greater dollar investment and has typically more than two decision makers. Because the dollar volume is higher, more is at risk for the buyer. Layers of decision makers help create a cushion for the risk. Take for example an accounting software product that costs over $1,000,000. Money and time invested in conversion and training people makes it imperative that the decision to purchase is fully vetted. The selling cycle in a complex sale tends to be longer than that in a simple sale.

When working with complex sales involving several buying influencers, you may find or already know an individual within the company or associated with the company that we call the Chauffeur. This individual becomes an all-important resource for you to gain the inside track to the buying influencers. Imagine the familiar chauffeur of the movies, who is privy by default to the back seat deals of executives and is trusted for their discretion. Their job rests in finding the shortcuts or back roads to avoid congestion or sometimes more importantly to protect the interests of their employer/client. They learn the individual habits of their patrons and can foretell preferences and avoid conflict. As the name implies, your Chauffeur will have the inside track and information to help you navigate through unfamiliar territory. Your chauffeur will offer tips and information that will enable you to identify the buying resources, pinpoint the specific objectives of each buying influencer in the purchase and show you how to deliver a product/service that produces a mutual advantage for both parties more easily. The Chauffeur has a vested interest in you and your company's earning the business. It is a mutually beneficial relationship.

For the sale in which there is no apparent Chauffeur to guide you, the salesperson must find the buying influencers without this guide. To assist with this process, I identify four Buying Influencers. They are called the Investigative Buyer, the Utilitarian Buyer, the Sensitive Buyer, and the Dominant Buyer. Each of the three buyers sees the world differently and has different roles and criteria for buying. If you have not met with these buyers before making a proposal, you are not on target and may be wasting time without the best information.

The Investigative Buyer gathers products/services information. This person may be from positions as diverse as purchasing, IT, engineering, or operations personnel. This individual does not usually offer up company information but is interested in gathering new product/service information for the purpose of qualifying or disqualifying the product/service. Price plays a role in the decision to qualify or disqualify. The Investigative Buyer cannot, alone, say yes to a product/service, and this individual can help maneuver you through the buying process.

The Utilitarian Buyer is the actual user of the product/service. These individuals can be often overlooked as players in the selling process. Because they use the product, it is essential that they understand the benefit and how to use it. A company I worked for designed plastic collapsible bins for the automotive after-market. These bins were replacing metal bins, and the forklift drivers who handled the bins insisted that the plastic bins would simply not hold up in the loading process with the forklift. To sell the plastic bin, our company worked to retrain the forklift drivers in the loading process. Instead of the sale being sabotaged by the drivers who typically rammed steel bins onto a pallet, we trained them in a different loading method, which was far simpler and took less time.

The Sensitive Buyer is directly affected by the product or service. This individual or group in the organization measures the product or service by the consistency of productivity. For example, if a ball bearing on the line is replaced by a cheaper product, and that line breaks down when the bearing fails, the Sensitive Buyer suffers the consequences. If the product or service consistently produces good results, the Sensitive Buyer will move you more quickly through the buying process. Though the people in this position cannot say yes to you, they can overrule the Investigative Buyers, especially when productivity diminishes due to product/service quality.

In the case of selling plastic bins, the Utilitarian Buyer may be the head of shipping. In the case of a software customer service/CRM solution, the Utilitarian Buyer may be VP of Technology Services. The person you work with is dependent on the type of company and sale. If you need assist sorting out just who the right buyer is for your project, contact us and we can help you.

Last is the Dominant Buyer. As is indicated by the title, this influencer dominates every other buying influencer involved in the buying process. This individual can be a manager, vice-president, president, COO, CFO,CEO, even a board member. This is the ultimate buying influencer, and this individual can say yes or no to the purchase. Though these individuals may consider the recommendations of the other Buying Influencers, they ultimately have the final say and the budget ownership. They can reject the product or service even when the others have said yes to you.

Now that we have their identities, how do we reach them without the aid of a Chauffeur? If your prospect alone is the only decision maker, you have no worries. You're in a simple sale. But even at that, what is the guarantee that you have reached the Dominant Buying Influencer? We teach salespeople to pose a direct question to the prospect, which will firm up the identity of the dominant Buying Influencer and perhaps produce others.

If your prospect offers up no other Buying Influencers and says he/she makes the decision, yet you are uncertain, a follow-up comment/question would be in order. These "soft" questions and comments to the prospect build on the trust and rapport already established, and it is much more likely that you will receive accurate information when using this technique. Many times, I hear prospects say they do run the decision by a boss, the president, board member, or committee.

How you reach these Buying Influencers and just how many of these Buying Influencers you communicate with personally will depend on the questions you ask of prospects and the information received from them. Even though a prospect may be a President, that individual may need or want to confer with others in the organization and perhaps may not wish to bring you into the mix. Committees can be especially threatening to upper management who don't wish to appear foolish or embarrassed if they cannot sufficiently answer their questions as to why your product/service is necessary to the company's operations. To avoid the problem of being kept out of the loop, I rehearse the prospect for the tough questions that may be asked regarding my products/services. By doing this, I gain well-rehearsed prospects who will be an advocate for me if I'm not present. Or the prospects may simply invite me to meet with the other Buying Influencers.

There will be times when you are working directly with a CEO or President and believe you have reached the Dominant Buyer. You may find that these individuals still take the purchasing process to another top management person. Titles don't always determine the Buying Influencers. The buying process in a complex sale can have several twists and turns. To avoid pitfalls and the possibility of being misled by company titles, we developed questions for prospects so that the salesperson can get a clear picture of the buying process within the organization.

- Do they have a specific buying process?

- Have they purchased a similar product/service before?

- If not, what would they have done had they been presented with a product/service such as this?

- What type of consensus is needed to decide to move the process forward?

- How long do they expect it to take?

- What is the latest date the project can be implemented?

- What might be an optimum date, considering the number of steps needed to go through the process?

- Which members of the buying influencer groups can approve to move forward?

- Is there a committee? Members?

- Is one committee member more influential?

- Historically, what is the pattern with committee purchasing?

- Will you speak with members of the committee?

How have the committee members interacted with one another in the past?

These questions serve to educate you on the company's purchasing process. There may be many people you pick up along the way, and this way can begin to resemble a maze. To untangle this maze, I encourage my salespeople to continue to ask question upon question of prospects. With each new buying influencer that enters the maze, use appropriate questions to ferret out the information that delivers not only the Dominant Buying Influencer but points to the path of the purchasing process.

Chapter Highlights

Chapter 5 Buying Influencers

Simple or complex sale determines your approach.

- Chauffeur: has a vested interest in your company earning the business.

- Investigative Buyer: gathers products /service information.

- Utilitarian Buyer: is the user of your product/service.

- Sensitive Buyer: is directly affected by results of the product or service.

- Dominant Buyer: dominates all other buying influencers and has the final decision or money power.

Chapter 6

RESOURCES

The salesperson's money fears.

We have reached the point in the sales conversation where we have uncovered the prospect's emotional reasons for buying, have identified the appropriate buying influencers, and are now faced with our next goal, which is to establish whether there are funds available to purchase our product or service. However, this is one of the most difficult areas for the salesperson. It sounds easy enough. Just ask if the company has the funds available to invest in your product or service. And how often have you balked at this point in the sales call? And why might that be? Do you still harbor an embarrassing memory of talking about someone else's money or worth? Are you afraid the prospects will be insulted if the question of available funds comes up? Shouldn't it simply be implied that the prospects are able to afford your product or service? After all, you were invited in to discuss products or services. But isn't it impolite for the salesperson to bring up money?

This may be the mindset of some individuals, so I'll teach you how to overcome those hesitancies.

Another reason for salespeople's inability to approach the money issue with a prospect is the belief they are not convinced of the value of the product or service they are selling. They may understand the working value of the product and may be afraid to discuss its worth with conviction in terms of the actual cost of the service or product. They do not want to be put in the position of defending the cost.

And finally, they may truly fear losing the business if the cost of the product or service is challenged. Do you really have the business until the money is in your pocket? Learn to be confident when defending the price of your product or service. Understand its value to the consumer/ your buyer(s), whose emotional response indicates a need for your service or product.

Terms

Too often, salespeople leave conversations about terms of payment to the accounting department. And because of this, the salesperson sees charge backs on their commission statements. How does this happen? It begins with the reticence to talk about money and consequently rolls over to a lapse in discussing the form of payment. It is so much easier to let the accounting department handle money collection. Of course, you are not the finance person; you merely collect the commission and do not worry about a payment plan for your client.

Here is what typically happens when a salesperson hands over the terms of payment to the accounting department instead of taking it up with the prospect. A company has a standard net 30-day payment plan and invoices the client. On the 45th day of the invoice, with no payment received, the dunning or collection letter goes out to the client. At 60 to 90 days past, the salesperson becomes involved and phones the client with a reminder that payment is 30 days net, and the client is now three months overdue. It is a rare occurrence when the client quickly follows up with payment. Instead, the salesperson is likely to hear the client complain that he did not have a conversation about your company's payment schedule. Where does the pressure fall? On the salesperson who has not defined his company's payment terms.

Suppose instead that the salesperson discussed terms during the conversation about resources. This conversation will have a different tone. Instead of the client accusing the salesperson with a "You didn't tell me that!" statement, the salesperson asks the question, "What should we do now?" The pressure to commit to payment is back on the shoulders of the client, where it should be. Tired of charge backs? We hope so because it is time you learn to take charge of the resources issue.

Starting a resource conversation

Now that you understand the salesperson's role in securing resource information and defining payment terms, how do you start the resource conversation?

Very simply, ask if there are resources available to fund this project. If you can put aside all the social taboos and muster the confidence you have in yourself and your product, you will find that there are three types of prospects that you will encounter: 1. Those who have budgets or funding, 2. Those who don't have budgets-Negative NOrman, and 3. Those who may have budgets but refuse to divulge the information --Negative Ned.

Though all these answers appear to be rather straightforward, further questioning by the salesperson reveals more complicated scenarios.

The prospect who has a budget

The answer is "Yes"!

The follow-up question is, "Can you tell me approximately how much that might be?" Up to this point, the salesperson has qualified the prospect based on the level of trust achieved during the rapport stage, uncovered the prospect's emotional reasons for buying, heard the prospect define the problem's financial cost to the company, and now can expect to hear that the prospect is willing to invest in the product or service being offered. If the prospect has $1000 available and your product is $900, your response is, "I think we may be able to work with that."

If, on the other hand, the cost of the product is $5000, the salesperson knows there isn't enough money for the product, and the sales call ends.

Remember, you, as the salesperson have invested the time of ONE sale call up to this point and can walk away now. Or you can further establish the financial qualifications of your candidate using the following comment.

"It doesn't sound as though you have enough resources to solve your problem."

If your prospect sincerely wants to solve the problem and indicates that finding resources is a possibility even though resources have not been budgeted, you can ask,

"Historically, what process did you or your company follow when you needed to find resources to pay for a solution?"

The salesperson will continue to question the prospect until the conversation reveals a clear understanding that resources can be secured, and the salesperson is comfortable with the direction the sales call is going. Further questions will lead you up the food chain while you learn who else may be involved in approving the resources.

The Negative NOrman or the prospects with no budget

This method of questioning can be applied to the second answer when the prospect says, "We don't have the budget to pay for your product or service." Why do we follow up with a prospect with no budget or resources? When a prospect has indicated a problem and appears to want to solve the problem, an assertive salesperson will follow up with, "You have a problem that you want to fix, so how were you hoping to fix it?"

If you hear from the prospect that resources are sometimes made available, you ask a question like the one in the previous budget paragraph. "Can you tell me approximately how much that might be and how has that worked the past?" That may well find you discovering new buying influencers that do lead to available resources. Under these conditions, the salesperson must be assured that there is a clear understanding of fund approval. If resources don't appear to be available, then the sales call ends.

Negative Ned or the prospect that may have a budget and is reluctant to reveal it.

A prospect with an unwillingness to divulge information is an even bigger roadblock in the sales call. When a prospect does not wish to give out any financial information, the salesperson must decide if the prospect might still be viable and, if so, continue the conversation based on an agreement to ask a couple more questions. And though you do not need an exact figure from the prospect, you do need to determine financial ability to purchase. You do not want to spend your limited and precious resource — time--in a sales call that goes nowhere for lack of financial resources. In response to this prospect's unwillingness or inability to divulge financial information, the salesperson uses a ballpark-figure process. The salesperson wants to find out if the prospect has financial resources within a certain ballpark of the product or service available. To coax a prospect to reveal his resources, the salesperson prompts,

"Well, of course I can understand that you may not be able to tell me your available resources, but for me to understand if I should still be here, is your financial resource availability in the ballpark of $900 to $1000?"

Hopefully you will get agreement and can follow up with,

"Right now, I'm not looking for an exact number. I'm just trying to figure out if I should be here or if there are others, I need to speak with to approve the funds."

If the prospect is willing to grant this information to a range of availability, the sales call moves forward. The salesperson may also find that the prospect will never have the resources and will let you go.

There are three different answers to the question, "Do you or your company have financial resources available to purchase our product/ service?" The stellar salesperson examines the possibilities of each answer supplied by a prospect and moves forward with questions appropriate to each answer. Stellar salespeople confident in their product/service will not be tempted to financially undersell just to make a sale and are usually fearless when asking a prospect if financial resources are available.

I had been working on a multimillion-dollar sale for three years with a Fortune 500 customer. The marketing team in the company had an emotional reason to buy, as their largest competitor had implemented a similar marketing solution sold by our company's largest competitor. The company claimed the competitive marketing program was the key reason they were losing sales and market share to the competitor. We implemented many trial programs, and after a three-year sales cycle they informed me, they were ready to go and that our solution had the buy off at the highest levels. I asked how much had been budgeted, and they replied, don't worry about it-this is a strategic initiative for the company.

OK, I thought, it's rock and roll time! – I will have earned a place on our company's sales incentive trip to Switzerland with my wife, and my name will be in lights with our company after three years of hard work. This was my biggest sale ever. I could tell my wife to go shop for the new car she wanted. This sale was done. They said it was a done deal and they had budget.

Then I realized I needed to find out who approved the budget. The COO of this $50B company said our solution was a strategic initiative. I asked if the CFO had approved the sale, and the reply was, "Don't worry about the CFO, we have this handled."

I dropped work on all other clients sales to ensure we locked up this massive sale. Once other decision makers were identified, I flew all over the country and met with other members of their marketing team.

I was certain we would get this big sale. We had a multi-media, $60k presentation just to make sure everyone attending the presentation was excited. Competition was invited in to ensure the company was receiving a fair price. We had internal coaches working with us on the presentation, and the day before, we had them preview and give feedback on the presentation. The T's were crossed and the I's dotted; or were they?

We presented, and it was a fantastic presentation. "You nailed it!" were the comments and feedback we received from the 30+ attendees at the presentation. I was so confident that I had the agreement drawn up and presented to the team at the end of the presentation, with an estimated budget, since I couldn't obtain a budget number from the prospect. They claimed they were unable to divulge the budget numbers. We all thought we should charge more than usual, since it had been such a long sales cycle and was a strategic initiative for the company.

Days went by, and we received no signed agreement; all we heard was that it was in legal in review. Finally, after eleven business days and feeling like I had been to hell and back and was now pessimistic about the business, we got a response. "The executive team didn't have a budget set aside and decided that the solution was too much of a me-too response and we needed something radically different to differentiate our company."

How did I invest so much and get nothing? **We didn't ever confirm the budget or resources**. In this case the only executive who was able to confirm a budget was the CFO, and we believed the people we did meet with when they said not to worry about the CFO because "they had it handled." We never met with the CFO.

In another project in the mid-1980's, we were working to develop a sales performance program for a large software company that sold through distributors. The program would motivate the distributors to sell more of the prospect's software. We tested the program with one distributor and initial results proved that for every dollar invested, the program produced over 200 for the company: that's over a 200 to 1 Return on Investment.

The prospect told me the results proved that this is a no-brainer sale and would be rolled out to the entire company. I announced the big sale to the executives in our company—the largest sale for our company that year. The software company needed to allocate budget to pay for the fixed costs to get the program going and pay for the first half-year before reaping the returns. My prospect had just one more sign-off with the executive team of the company. The prospect said again that it was a no-brainer and just a formality and that everyone on the executive team endorsed the program. I believed the prospective client.

The prospect presented to the executive team on a Thursday, and I didn't hear from him until the next Tuesday. The opening words from him were, "Wow, I was blindsided." That didn't sound like an approval of the big sale. "I have bad news," he went on, "the CEO and CFO said we need an employee cafeteria in our Silicon Valley facility and must take the money earmarked for the initiative and put it into the employee cafeteria." How did that happen? A solid ROI improves company sales and they put in an employee cafeteria! Yes, it is a true story.

I clearly did not meet with all the Buying Influencers to find out that no resources were ever really allocated to my company's program. Why? Because I didn't ask to meet with all buyers of the program or ask if budget was allocated to begin the program.

Chapter Highlights

Chapter 6 Resources

Identify the type of prospect(s) you encounter:

1-Those with a budget

- Ask further questions.

- Qualify that there is sufficient budget for your company's solution.

  2 - Negative NOrman-those with no budget

- Ask questions to determine how to fix the problem or find out why you are meeting.

- Attempt to discover new buying influencers.

  3 - Negative Ned-those who may have a budget and are unwilling to divulge the budget.

- Ask for a ballpark budget.

- Determine if it is worthwhile to you and the prospect to continue discussions.

Chapter 7

PRE-PRESENTATION AGREEMENT-PPA

Most salespeople make the mistake of not putting in place a Pre-Presentation Agreement--PPA. Without the PPA, the salesperson risks getting stuck in radio silence and losing control of the sale. This is a critical chapter for every salesperson.

In Chapter Two, we stated that the value of any product or service a salesperson brings to the marketplace is equivalent to GOLD. Though its actual cost to the client may be anywhere from $100 to more than a $10,000,000, if that product/service can solve a problem for a client, it's value to the client is much greater than the dollar figure attached to it. Traditional selling models build the features and benefits presentation into the initial phase of the sales call giving the prospect almost immediate access to the salesperson's GOLD (see note on pg. 23). One of the biggest missteps a salesperson can make is giving away the GOLD. Until a prospect is completely qualified, the prospect does not get access to the salesperson's GOLD. There needs to be a clear understanding of the prospect's ERB, a complete list of the buying influences, and sufficient resources and payment terms for the product/services.

By giving away the GOLD with a features and benefits presentation before completely qualifying the prospect, the salesperson ends up in a defensive position, haggling price, or in no position, with doors closing behind them. The salesperson loses control of the sale. Being certain to qualify the prospect is critical to the outcome of the sale and to the salesperson's maintaining control of the sale. In the previous chapters we outlined the methods for qualifying prospects.

- Establish Rapport, gauging the time wisely.

- Determine the ERB.

- Put in place a strong Meeting Agenda.

- Determine the Buying Influencers.

- Mutually agree on the handling of Future Communications.

- Discuss Resources and Payment Terms.

At the final stage of qualifying the prospect, the salesperson is ready to deliver the solution with a well-prepared presentation of the product or service. The salesperson is ready to deliver the GOLD. But hold it. Not so fast. I see the salesperson as still in the READY – FIRE – AIM position. And you are probably thinking, "What else is there? I've covered all my bases. The prospect is financially qualified, and payment terms have been outlined."

There is one final item in the sales call arsenal to be employed before the salesperson delivers the GOLD. It is called the PRE-PRESENTATION AGREEMENT. Again, you are probably thinking, "I've had conversations to uncover the ERB. The Meeting Agenda is agreed upon. Financial resources are clearly available. I've checked my list and covered everything. Now what? Haven't I learned all the information necessary to close the opportunity ?"

Throughout the qualifying process, the salesperson continually re-confirms all the points from the oral or written agenda and gets agreement from the prospect on those points. The prospect(s) hears herself/himself give the "OK" to what has been agreed or understood. By revisiting each qualifier with the prospect(s), the salesperson creates a Feedback Loop that each party hears. Consider that 90% of the time spent in front of the prospect is in oral communications, which in turn means that most of the agreements reached between the prospect and salesperson are oral agreements.

It may seem redundant to some to use the Feedback Loop at this point but think of the number of times in conversations with individuals that YOU have asked for clarification of points or expansion of ideas. It is not unusual for any of us to forget or misunderstand specific points of agreement during oral communications. Though we all attempt to hear what another is saying, at the same time we often have thoughts and questions forming in our minds ready to be asked or exchanged when our next opportunity to speak occurs. We may miss another's point here or there in the conversation. We may selectively listen for information important to us and miss a point valuable to the other party.

The PPA is the last opportunity to employ the Final Feedback Loop before the presentation. The salesperson revisits each step in the sales call with the prospect to be certain the prospect has a clear understanding of what has been stated and agreed upon and more importantly has not forgotten any key points. This PPA further reinforces the likelihood that the meeting agreements will be kept, and the sale will go through. Both the salesperson and the prospect are given the opportunity to clarify any points they may not have understood or include anything that may have been left out of the agreement. Without the PPA, the salesperson continues to withhold the GOLD.

The PPA has seven steps that create a loop of information from the prospect(s) back to the salesperson. At any point in the PPA the salesperson or the prospect(s) could correct, clarify, or expand the verbal/written agreement.

Review the emotional reasons for buying.

Confirm the financial resources are available to buy.

Revisit the agreement with the prospect to either decline or accept the offer.

The salesperson is always searching for more emotional reasons for buying-ERBs. When we have been asked why the salesperson might need more ERBs, we always reply that we have never had a student come to me to say he just lost the deal because he got too many ERBs. It is also possible for a new buying influencer to enter the picture. It is better now for the salesperson to have the information of another buying influencer than to be surprised later when the sale falls apart because that buying influencer is not on board.

Prospects can be fickle when money/ability to buy is discussed, so terms of payment need to be nailed down and be clear to all parties. Even after confirming agreement on all these important areas, the prospect still could decline the salesperson's offer. A prospect is always ready to put up barriers when dealing with a salesperson. The prospect removes that barrier of "being taken to the mat" by an aggressive salesperson when given permission to decline an offer of a product/service. From the prospect's perspective, the product or service may NOT be what is expected. It is important for both the prospect and the salesperson to be OK hearing "no thanks."

If a prospect does not plan either way, opting instead for more time to think about it, what should be the salesperson's next move? The assertive salesperson sees this tactic as prospect manipulation and calls them on it. By questioning the prospect on exactly what they need to think about, the salesperson is likely to hear that the prospect:

- Doesn't want to buy and is trying to be nice.

- May be trying to get more information.

- Is still skeptical.

- May not be able to make a buying decision.

- May not have the resources to buy.

- May be afraid to make a buying decision.

Or the salesperson may not have the true ERB. If one of these roadblocks to a sale crops up, the salesperson needs to dig deeper. "Can we expand on that?" If another issue is discovered, it can be determined then whether the sales call can go forward or if it will end. The PPA is a critical element in the selling process. It reinforces and confirms the many oral or written agreements made in the sales interview. It lets the prospect see you as an active listener. It clears the way for the prospect to say no and reduces the likelihood of a "think it over." In closing, the rule is NO PRE-REPRESENTATION AGREEMENT-NO GOLD.

Recently I was working with a digital marketing company to start up their sales. We had a sale that was in the bag at Big Software Company. The digital marketing company founders had given free trial copies of its product to the Big Software company and had announced to the Board of Directors and me that these sales were ready to be closed. They had zealous advocates of the company's products. At Big Software, the VP of Technology was the advocate and would filter news to us about the selling process at Big Software. His stated emotional reason for buying was that it would allow the Big Software Company to drive efficiencies out of recent company acquisition and provide a new product for Big Software to sell. As I got to know the VP, it was apparent that this wasn't an emotional reason for buying at all, and he wanted to throw some new initiatives out to prove his value and save his job. Clearly, I didn't understand the ERB and didn't have a precise picture of the financial implications of the sale. It also meant I hadn't confirmed that financial resources were available. I began to dig into the sale and identify other parties at Big Software who would be affected by the decision. We had yet to present the solution to the executive team or Dominant Buyer.

The VP wasn't introducing me, so I began setting up meetings on my own when I realized that I had yet to confirm and meet with all Buying Influencers and that they had no knowledge of my company's digital marketing solution. It had the potential of billing $15 million per year. This company kept running a no-cost trial program with our company just to keep me coming around and buying lunch for them. We had built the framework for the sale based on the client's word that we would get the business-we told the client about all the secret sauce, intellectual property, or GOLD of the business, and in turn they promised we would get the business when that big day came for the executive presentation. And by the way, there will be fourteen people from all over the country that will be part of the presentation. Don't worry though, we have your backs (according to the VP), and—we are the only ones that matter in this decision.

The format for the presentation was based on the digital marketing and the secret sauce or GOLD from us. Oh no, I thought-some clients pay money for this work, and did they send this information to our competitor? Yes, they had. I was upset, as we had given that to them in confidence, yet they shared it with a competitor.

According to my contact "Don't worry, just present your recommendations. The approval is just a formality. You needn't meet with the other executives."

A week went by and no word from the client, always a bad sign. Another two days, no word. I called, and client said, "Oh, nothing to worry about, we needed to invite in a competitor just to ensure we get a fair price-standard company purchasing practices. Don't worry. You have the business. I know you have contacted other people in our company, and I will take care of you."

I called back two days later. "Hey, my trusted friend, what is the budget?" I had yet to establish there were available resources.

My prospect responded, "You need to come back with your best offer. That is part of the process."

"Will you give a ballpark budget amount to me?" I asked.

"You come back with your best price."

"Is $2-5 million in the range?"

"I guess so," he responded.

"Great," I said. "Our Company has been working on this for two years so it must be at least $2 million—I can accept the range." They did sound a bit sketchy and uncertain though.

Two weeks before the presentation I had lunch with my friends at Big Software Company who are taking care of my business, and they promised this will be a sale. We brought in their boss who can sign the checks and approve the budget, just to be certain that base is covered. He told me some news. My competitors are flying around and meeting with everyone on the presentation committee. And why wouldn't they? They have nothing to lose. "Don't worry though," he says, "my team has told me this business is yours."

Wow, this felt weird. My insiders had told me not to bother meeting with them. The CEO of my company even said it's wasteful to go meet with them and spend all the company money. He said, "We earned this business, and if that's what it takes, we don't want their business." I was feeling very uneasy and queasy by now.

I added three people from my team on the day of the presentation from our company as a show of force. We laid out our recommendations, or GOLD, which is what the RFP is based on. The presentation went well, seemed to be smooth, lots of head nods. They knew we deserved this business and that we understood their company. The business was ours. Maybe.

Two days of waiting after the presentation, and I was still waiting for the call. Should I go to lunch and miss it? Friday afternoon at 2 p.m. and still no call. At 2:17 p.m. the phone rang, and it was the Big Software client. I was exhilarated and ready to accept the business, the big order.

They started out by saying, "You understand our business, and it was a great presentation. Your competitor gets the business." I felt betrayed and lied to and felt they stole our ideas. How could that be their response?

"You were outsold," he told me. "Your competitor took your ideas and made them even better. They met with everyone on the committee, flew all over the country and their presentation addressed each individual and what their needs were. It was the bestselling I have seen. Sorry about that."

There was only one consolation. My competitor never got the business because the budget was never approved. Within a month the VP and EVP of Big Software had left the company, and when I met with the Big Software COO, I discovered he had never been in favor of the initiative.

Unfortunately, that company's false assurances about this sale to our Board of Directors without a Pre-Presentation Agreement led to my departure and to that company's eventual demise.

Another time, in another job I was calling on a major auto company in Detroit and working to get in position for a big sale in the fourth quarter to wrap up the year.

I had met with all the buyers and Buying Influencers and had a clear understanding of the financial implications. They had agreed to say no or yes and had confirmed the emotional reason for buying, which was to be perceived as further ahead than their automotive competitors by consumers and their competitors. Prior to presenting, we had confirmed a budget amount. The client said they might say no if the budget wasn't approved, although they believed it would be approved, and typically it had been approved in the past. We also had met with the budget approver. They all liked our solution and said they would approve the budget. I found the actual budget approver by asking the manager I had been working with, who gave me a heads-up on the budget question. That question I asked to gain that introduction was, "If you like our solution, what happens then?" He said I would need to meet with the budget approver. I told my contact that if he wanted the benefits of our solution, he would need to arrange and attend the meeting with the budget approver and me. In the meeting with the budget approver, I prepped the manager and had him state his financial implications and emotional reason for buying.

I then asked the budget approver if he allocated the budget for our solution, and he said yes. I asked if he would say no if there wasn't a match. He stated that from all he heard, it sounded like there was a match. So, I said it sounded like a yes and I asked him if there were anyone else that we needed to meet with or any other issues that could stop this from being approved and what were the next steps? He replied that it would take about three weeks for the budget to be allocated to us. We scheduled a follow-up meeting and lunch three weeks later.

The prospect /Senior Vice President said the budget was approved, we sat down to lunch. and he filled out the order form. I had the CEO of our company with me, and he said that was the easiest sale he had ever seen. It was because I went through the PPA with the prospect, and then they found additional budget dollars. They had only allocated a smaller budget for our company and now had an additional $250,000 that had to be spent with our company by year's end. The PPA helped to secure the sale, and by securing the sale we were in the right place at the right time to receive more from their budget.

Chapter Highlights

Chapter 7 Pre-Presentation Agreement (PPA)

- Review the emotional reasons for buying.

- Confirm the financial implications of the problem.

- Confirm that financial resources are available to buy.

- Get an agreement from the prospect to say "no" if the product/ service does not solve the problem.

- Get an agreement from the prospect to say "yes' if the product does solve the problem.

- Take it as a "no," if prospect asks to think it over.

- Make an agreement for ongoing communications.

Chapter 8

THE PRESENTATION

In the first chapter, we laid out the six-step format for sales' calls and now have arrived at the sixth step. This is the moment most salespeople anticipate and relish. The salesperson is ready to offer the solution to the problem and put an end to the prospect's pain.

Up to this point in the sales process, the salesperson has not spent a great deal of time talking about the product or service. The job in the initial stages of the selling process has been mainly to obtain information about the prospect emotional reasons for buying, discovering the buying influences, and knowing the availability of resources.

Now it's time to deliver the GOLD. The salesperson schedules a presentation time, collects the needed materials, and allows sufficient time for review of the pre-presentation agreement and follow-up questions from the prospect.

The presentation typically focuses on the features and benefits of the product or service offered. However, features and benefits are often numerous, and not all may necessarily apply specifically to the prospect's problem. The salesperson that has learned the prospect's emotional reasons for buying is going to carefully tailor the presentation to maximize the impact to the prospect of the product's solution to the-ERB.

Take for example a prospect that is purchasing a new car. The salesperson points out several features on a car, focusing on a particular model with the highest-rated air-conditioning unit. The prospect announces that he's taking the car to Barrow, Alaska, and has no need for the unit and is unlikely to pay extra for a feature that will have little or no value to them in that climate. By pointing out those features that have little value to the prospect before determining what the prospect's reasons for buying were, the salesperson has lost the buyer and sale.

The salesperson is ready and has worked hard to reach this step in the process. So just prior to the actual presentation, I teach my students to re-confirm all the points in the pre-presentation and to listen carefully for any Early Warning Indicators, EWI, that may pop up. If any appear, I tell them to settle the matter before moving on to the presentation, to avoid what happened to the over-eager car salesperson. Now is the time to deal with any issue that might stall the sale. When the prospect confirms again that he is ready for the solution, the salesperson is ready to make the presentation and begins with the question,

"Which of the issues affecting the business would you like to address first?"

Sometimes a reminder or refresher is required for busy executives. Did they mention that saving money was an important issue or that adding the new software with a 10 to 1 ROI is important? Are those the issues affecting their business that they would like to address first, has that changed, or are there other priorities and issues?

By giving the prospect the opportunity to prioritize the ERB issues, the salesperson allows a sense of control to move to the prospect. And the salesperson's presentation then hits the specific ERB points outlined by the prospect. The presentation stays focused on only those points specific to this sale.

After the presentation, we ask, "Based on the information just presented, are you completely satisfied that we could solve this problem for you?"

If there is any hesitation or they are less than completely satisfied, we ask, "Help me understand what would make you completely satisfied?" It may be that we need to spend more time answering questions, but I want to know while I am still in front of the prospect that this solution is bought . Spending this time now eliminates a stall.

When the time has come to close, I ask one last question, "would you like our support?" And then I stop talking.

Chapter Highlights

Chapter 8 The Presentation

- Tailor the presentation to maximize the impact of the product's solution to client's pain.

- Ask, "Which of the issues affecting the business would you like to address first?'

- Determine, based on the information presented, is the prospect completely satisfied that we can solve this problem?

- Finish with, "Would you like our support?"

Chapter 9

CONFIRMATION

The new customer has done all the research, listened to all the competitors, and made the final decision to buy. The anticipation and excitement of purchasing a solution or new product to influence the bottom line has the customer riding a new high. This is often a short-lived high, though, before buyers' remorse rears its ugly head and the salesperson finds themselves with a handwringing customer, questioning his recent investment. To avoid this practically inevitable occurrence, the salesperson must address these second thoughts immediately, and confirm the sale once again.

Buyer's Remorse

The salesperson understands that their product or service is not perfect, and the customer at the time of purchase believes it is. Before the customer faces buyer's remorse, the salesperson asks the customer to reflect on his decision to purchase. When re-examining the decision with the customer, a successful salesperson tends to ask questions such as:

"What do you see as its greatest benefit? Where does it fit in your company? How will it be accepted? Why will it be useful? Are there any drawbacks to the product? Can you overcome the drawbacks? Will the drawbacks be significant? How will you address concerns, if any?

Asking these questions will ensure the sale stays intact.

Ward Off the Competition

Business does not exist without competition. Your competition is at your heels every day, which means that your prospect is also forced to deal with the competition. In most cases, the competition invariably works to dislodge your sale. My goal to secure the sale relies on my ability to support the prospect be comfortable and confident when approached by the competition. The salesperson asks the customer to tell why he bought from us. By telling why they bought from us, he reinforce their own buying decision. This in turn allows them to become less vulnerable to the inevitable attack from the competition.

Not all prospects need assistance in dealing with the competition but preparing those who may be less confident when standing up to the competition further assures a confirmation of the sale.

Early in my career I was selling Performance Programs to companies. These were incentives and training programs. We competed for six months on an opportunity to train and deliver a training program to employees at a major Hotel Company delivering world-class guest or customer service. What was behind the large initiative is that Hotel Company was positioning the company for sale and wanted to show they had world-class guest services. Our company was small and relatively unknown, and we were competing with some of the most renowned training companies. There was a committee of six people responsible for the decision. There was a new executive responsible for HR who was the key decision maker or Dominant Buyer; she also brought in a cadre of people she worked with in previous companies, after the sale was made to the executive team. These people were very interested in making a name for themselves. Our sale was very much driven by the influence of the relationship I had with the executive team, not the HR team. And at the time it appeared that the HR team went along with that team's decision to choose our company, albeit reluctantly.

I met with the team responsible for the implementation of the initiative and asked why they are doing business with our company. They said they were told to work with us and could do this project themselves. Our assumption was that despite their reluctance, we had cover from the executive team, and the VP of Sales said, "Let's get going—we need the revenue." When I asked what they would like from the solution that we had yet to present or what wasn't perfect about our solution, the implementation group said, "We need to be more involved." No problem, I thought, a very active client.

When I asked what they would say if any of our competitors came back, they stated, "We won't be working with any other outside firm."

We received a letter of intent and began our work with the hotel chain to design and build a world-class training program. I was traveling to Kansas City for the program kick-offs in the first week and received a call that the program was being pulled. The HR implementation team didn't see the value in the price tag and was pulling the program and would do it all themselves. I pleaded and cajoled, but no one in the company could turn it around.

I neglected to understand the importance of the new team and failed to convince them of the value of working with our group. I heard them tell me that they would bring the business in-house. Our company had over $100,000 in expenses and a lot of my time and got no business. In this case I didn't understand the competition was internal resources. We didn't sell the value to the entire team, which was changing and didn't really understand or want to understand the importance of confirmation in an agreement. In addition, we did not confirm an agreement that they would pay us in a timely manner for our services.

Chapter Highlights

Chapter 9 Confirmation

- Buyer's Remorse-prevents the buyer from changing their mind.

- Warding Off the Competition prevents the competition from getting back in with customer and stealing the sale from you.

- The sale is not complete until you have delivered your product or service and the money is in your bank account or digital currency.

Chapter 10

Technology And Business Development

Salespeople will be needed, and the following will be needed, however, to be successful, read the book, and subscribe to our newsletters. Follow a proven sales process, as you have read in this book and stay ahead of the technology with a view to how it impacts your business. We will provide data and a view to the future .

Here is some information before we move on:

90 % of human communication is non-verbal. Technology cannot do what we can do in a human interaction.

You can be more successful fully utilizing technology .

Communicating with the most qualified prospects

Gaining insights into what specifically is of interest to prospects.

Automation of sales processes, cold calls/outreach, standard prospect and client communication, customer support…

What does it mean to you? More time and more money

As an individual responsible for revenue generation, technology will have more of an impact on you than ever before, what is coming will make your head spin. *My objective is to provide information for you and me to make educated choices about how technology impacts our future career and successes.*

This is an addition to our book from 2013 as technology has impacted our careers and this is an update to make the book current, as well as providing an ongoing newsletter for revenue generation professionals. As

I dove into research, it is a dramatic, accelerated pace of change. I am absolutely blown away by what's ahead and suggest that you subscribe to the newsletter below to stay current on changes after this book:

Jamesbhayden.com

During the past two years, I have been utilizing marketing intelligence, campaign management and other sales tracking CRM software. All these tools have improved sales processes and efficiency, we have found utilizing AI reduces sales costs by 40% and improved closing ratios by 20+%. Then, I discovered AI and how it's impacted our work today and likely will impact how you approach business. Hang onto your hats, it's going to be a fun ride!

Its every day now:

- Artificial Intelligence to create 58 million new jobs by 2022.
- The AI industry could be worth more than $15 trillion by 2030.
- AI industry will be generating revenues of $118.6 billion a year by 2025.
- 86% of executives at fast-growing companies say AI is important to their comp success.

Goldman Sachs predicts that 2/3 of all jobs globally will be impacted by AI and AI will increase global GDP by 7%.

It's no wonder, then, that the likes of Bill Gates, the co-founder of Microsoft, has called it "as fundamental" as inventions like the personal computer, the Internet, and the mobile phone.

What about my job and life? More later. Will we be slaves to the machines in the next twenty years? Maybe, and more later how to take control.

Will AI usurp the roles of revenue generation professionals or enhance what we do? Yes, to both, let's prepare together. More to follow.

HOLY CRAP-are you ready to really harness technology? The world of revenue generation is a new world and as my first boss said *"**Adapt or die** "*. AI can be your personal assistant and generate personalized outreach and set qualified meetings-TODAY YES in bold again-TODAY!

Picture a meal with six courses, with conversation and discussion. Your questions will be discussed, you will have nutrition and fulfillment in an environment of people with interesting thoughts and questions. This will be covered in the upcoming newsletters.

Let's eat - this will be like being at a friend's house for dinner, when they are cooking a six-course meal…first course will be what is AI history and definition, second course will be what is simmering today, third course will be why is technology and AI important in your world, fourth course is what your work and life will look like, fifth course is what the timeframe is for these changes; sixth course, dessert, is a roadmap.

There will be new additions to the meal every week in the newsletter. Jamesbhayden.com

I am suggesting the newsletter in addition to the book as the chapter is written and done and the newsletter will provide current updates.

There will be new additions to the meal every week. What do you want to know and what would like to consume? This menu will be driven by your requests and with the intention of preparing you for what is ahead.

Ok, let's dig in now.

Today customers utilize blogs, websites, and articles, and then a company can determine if someone is interested in their product by how much time they spend and where they click. For example, I was looking at cars today; I clicked on the car I was interested in. In 20 minutes, a salesperson sent a personalized video and a text.

Most consumers and businesspeople give up personal information for the data on a website, blog, or link. When this occurs the company then has your contact information and browsing data and may even buy more information on you from other sources.

With sales tools like Zoom Info or Sixth Sense; I can find 80% of people I am targeting and contact them by business and personal e-mail, mobile and sometimes home landline number.

In addition, I can find their hobbies, interests, family, pets ...before I even speak with them.

The following content will cover why salespeople are required, what todays salesperson looks like, and the tools, people and other resources required for success.

John Naisbitt in Megatrends coined the term High Tech, High Touch. The more we adopt and embrace technology the greater the need for human interaction /touch. Some behavioral scientists claim we require at least twelve human touches a day to maintain mental health. Seems like the acceleration of technology will diminish human to human interaction.

For this meal, we will be begin serving a first course now. What is AI and its history? Subsequent newsletters will round out the meal, as we look for more spices and our palettes become more sophisticated and change. In the meantime, please send any questions.

First course, what is AI-a history and definition. AI -it's not steak sauce! (One person asked what all the fuss is about AI, it's just good steak sauce).

Let's dig in and uncomplicate this technology coming up.

Artificial Intelligence (AI) is a field that combines computer science and data to enable machines to perform tasks that require human intelligence[1]. AI systems can perceive their environment, reason, learn, and take actions that maximize their goals[1]. AI can manifest in different forms and applications, such as expert systems, machine learning, and deep learning[12]. AI can also simulate or approximate human cognitive skills, such as problem-solving, meaning discovery, and generalization[13].

Here is what Wikipedia says about the history of Artificial Intelligence:

The **history of artificial intelligence** (**AI**) began in antiquity, with myths, stories and rumors of artificial beings endowed with intelligence or consciousness by master craftsmen. The seeds of modern AI were planted by philosophers who attempted to describe the process of human thinking as the mechanical manipulation of symbols. This work culminated in the invention of the **programmable digital computer** in the 1940s, a machine based on the abstract essence of mathematical reasoning. This device and the ideas behind it inspired a handful of scientists to begin seriously discussing the possibility of building an electronic brain.

The field of AI research was founded at a workshop held on the campus of Dartmouth College, USA during the summer of 1956.[1] Those who attended would become the leaders of AI research for decades. Many of them predicted that a machine as intelligent as a human being would exist in no more than a generation, and they were given millions of dollars to make this vision come true.[2]

Eventually, it became obvious that commercial developers and researchers had grossly underestimated the difficulty of the project.[3] In 1974, in response to the criticism from **James Lighthill** and ongoing pressure from congress, the US and **British Governments** stopped funding undirected research into artificial intelligence, and the difficult years that followed would later be known as an "AI winter". Seven years later, a visionary initiative by the **Japanese Government** inspired governments and industry to provide AI with billions of dollars, but by the late 80s the investors became disillusioned and withdrew funding again.

Investment and interest in AI boomed in the first decades of the 21st century when **machine learning** was successfully applied to many problems in academia and industry due to new methods, the application of powerful computer hardware, and the collection of immense data sets.

AI has been with us for some time, think of calculators and predictive text on your phone. When calculators were allowed in school many math teachers protested, claiming the end of critical mathematical thought.

Why all the buzz about AI now? AI has been developing for the longest time, what is different today and why are so many technology leaders worried? For the first time, massive leaps in data processing speeds and bandwidth have led to this acceleration of technology. Early stages of quantum computing are just beginning. **See end of the chapter for more about quantum computing, if interested.**

Ok, there is change coming, it's here; we have dealt with change like no humans have dealt with **ever!**

Let's look at how we humans deal with technology change to gain insights into the changes coming our way.

How humans have dealt with technology change:

Throughout history we humans have resisted change, when barcodes were introduced, many religious leaders believed it was the sign of the antichrist; when calculators and the internet was forming, many educators went on strike and predicted the end of critical thinking. The New York Times reported that productivity was stable throughout the adoption of the Internet. Workers are more productive, and the productivity gain was offset by leisurely browsing the web.

Here is a story, generated by AI:

"Once upon a time, there was a small village that was known for its traditional ways of living. The villagers were happy with their simple lives and were content with what they had. One day, a new technology was introduced to the village that promised to make their lives easier and more comfortable.

At first, the villagers were hesitant to try out this new technology as they were afraid of change and didn't want to lose their traditional ways of living. However, some of them were curious and decided to give it a try.

As more and more people started using this new technology, rumors began to spread about its negative effects on health and well-being. People started getting anxious and fearful about the consequences of using this new technology.

The village elders decided to hold a meeting to discuss the issue and come up with a solution. After much debate, they decided to conduct research on this new technology and its effects on health.

The research showed that while there were some negative effects associated with this new technology, it also had many benefits that could improve their lives significantly. The villagers realized that they had been too quick to judge this new technology without fully understanding it.

In the end, the villagers embraced this new technology and learned how to use it safely and responsibly. They realized that change can be scary, and it can also bring about positive changes if approached with an open mind."

When a new technology is introduced, people tend to have concerns about its impact on their lives. Some of these concerns include psychological, social, and health issues that may arise from overuse of technology such as eyestrain and difficulty focusing on important tasks[1]. People may also resist new technologies when they perceive that the benefits of new technologies will only accrue to a small section of society, while the risks are likely to be widespread[2]. It is important to think through the ethics of new technology before there's a problem[3]. Concerns multiply as artificial intelligence (AI) and machine-learning technologies begin to nudge aside humans, assuming greater roles in running our economy, transportation, defense, medical care, and personal lives

The amount of information disseminated today compared to 1975 is staggering; some say from the beginning of recorded time until 1975 is the amount of recorded information is what is disseminated in a two-day period now.

The total amount of information created on the world's electronic devices is expected to surpass the zettabyte mark this year (a barely conceivable 1 with 21 zeroes after it)[1].

Over the past 30 years, journalism in the United States has gradually shifted towards more opinion-based content that appeals to people's emotions and relies heavily on argumentation and less on factual reporting[2]. Cable television's new 24-hour news cycle brought major changes. It meant newsrooms didn't have longer periods of time to prepare content, check it, edit it, vet it, and then present it to audiences.

Ouch, that's some big change-how to adapt is the challenge.

Here is an analogy, as a thought starter for now:

I have enjoyed car racing at a track and have attended car racing schools, which is really an advanced driver safety school. One of my favorite life and business analogies comes from car racing school. There is a drill where you slalom around cones for one mile, increasing the speed five miles per hour (mph) each time/lap from 30 to 60 mph. The real challenge is there is a person at the end of the mile with a red flag and each time the flag is raised you must skip the next cone. What does all that mean? The drill is a skill that a race driver must develop a vision to see what is coming at them immediately while keeping an eye on the distance to ensure upcoming events aren't impacting the driver in the future. Pay attention to what's in front of you, with a watchful eye to what is developing in the future. There is nothing more apt than what is happening to us today except we begin at 100 mph rather than 30 mph.

Maybe, we needn't be so worried…or more worried?

AI specially CHAT GPT did the heavy lifting for some of the updates for this book. AI will also be responsible for more misinformation, propaganda, and scams that we have ever seen. Buckle up, read on and let's focus on the impact on our work world.

Social media and marketing are very effective now in generating revenue for companies. Much more content to come.

Our sales methodology and approach previously were based on communication by phone, e-mail, and landline phone. Since we published the first edition of the book e-mail has been a preferred communications form. Now fewer than 20% of emails are opened. 95% of text messages in the US are opened within five minutes. Text is the most effective communications today, for the most part.

AI is scary and unknown for many of us. The intention of the newsletters will be to demystify the technology for you; highlight current developments and provide insights into possible courses of action to prepare and possibly stay ahead of all the changes. Change is a constant in our world and being prepared seems to be an imperative to stay up with changes and even developing insights that may lead to unique niches for you. Robert Browning "A man [and woman's) reach should exceed their grasp." And some of us may feel constant irritation and turmoil from all the technology. A reminder-one of the most beautiful of nature's creations is the pearl. The pearl is created by constant friction. Let's work together to minimize the irritation.

Second course: what is simmering today.

Technology has enabled companies to better understand their customers in many ways. The data technology available today gives businesses unprecedented abilities when it comes to understanding their customers. By combining transactional, demographic, and attitudinal data from internal and external sources, companies can predict what customers want more accurately and make sure they're in the right place at the right time to provide them[1]. Some current technologies are Zoom Info, Hub Spot, Salesforce, Outreach, Linked-In and others.

Moreover, companies using artificial intelligence have access to data from their customers in their systems, to understand the customer and to make improvements to the customer experience and product. Customer experience involves a variety of factors that can be analyzed by AI[2].and other technologies.

For example, when working with a trade/service industry business, customers commonly aren't sure when the business' staff will turn up to complete the service. Companies can effectively utilize technology to bridge this gap by increasing communication via automated messages and so on, thus resulting in a better customer experience[3].

Understanding your customers' current and shifting needs starts with a mix of effective customer listening approaches such as voice of the customer (VoC), defining personas, developing customer journey maps, and inspiring more customer-centric decisions — all critical factors in achieving the goal of better understanding and adapting to customer needs....[4].

Technology and AI have a massive impact on revenue generation. The abundance of online information has made it easier for consumers to educate themselves about purchases, which has led to a shift in the way business consumers purchase products and services. With the rise of online shopping, there is less need for human intervention in the purchasing process. Sales professionals can gather incredible data about an individual buyer and the reasons, strategic initiatives, why a company will buy a product or services using AI[12]. AI can streamline the sales process by using extremely detailed data on individuals, including real-time geolocation data, to create highly personalized product or service offers. Later in the journey, AI assists in upselling and cross-selling and can reduce the likelihood that customers will abandon their digital shopping carts[2].

Learn more:

hbr.org2. hbr.org3. entrepreneur.com4. bcg.com5. entrepreneur. com6. mckinsey.com7. cuseum.com8. smartinsights.com9. blog.hubspot. com10. ucf.edu11. thinkific.com12. elearningindustry.com13. statista. com14. ucf.edu15. saleshacker.com+11 more

Sales has changed quite a bit in recent years, thanks to new technological developments and a general shift in attitudes regarding how customers make purchasing decisions. Advances in technology have drastically changed the way consumers shop, both in-store and online. The past decade has seen a rise of direct-to-consumer brands and companies built nearly entirely on social media. Offline stores began experimenting with new forms of tech to entice shoppers back into brick-and-mortar stores[12].

Mobile technology has transformed the buying experience. Customers can research, evaluate, and purchase products and services online using this technology. Social media has also played a significant role in sales. Companies are using social media to reach out to customers, build brand awareness, develop leads/interest and drive sales[3].

Salespeople are using technology to streamline their sales techniques and the sales process. From prospecting to closing, today's mobile, social, big data, and cloud technologies are revamping the sales process in ways that would have been unthinkable only a few decades ago[3].

In terms of people, sales teams are becoming more specialized, and data driven. Salespeople are using data to identify potential customers, personalize their sales presentations , and track their progress[3].

In conclusion, technology has changed the sales process in many ways over the last decade. It has transformed the way consumers shop, the way salespeople sell, and the way companies market their products and services[312].

Learn more:

businessinsider.com2. dataclarity.uk.com3. salesforce.com4. salesforce. com5. forbes.com6. bdc.ca7. conga.com8. businessinsider.com9. conga. com10. forbes.com11. weforum.org12. weforum.org13. forbes.com14. weforum.org15. pewresearch.org— see less.

Here's a story by AI about how AI is impacting sales and marketing jobs:

"Once upon a time, sales and marketing jobs were done manually by humans. And with the advent of AI, things have changed drastically. AI has revolutionized marketing and sales by increasing efficiency and streamlining procésses[1]. For example, AI tools like ChatGPT can assist create and execute content such as emails and taglines much faster than traditional methods[1].

AI can also assist improve sales processes by reducing call time by 60-70% and realizing cost reductions of 40-60%[2]. Companies using AI in sales were able to increase their leads by more than 50%[2]."

AI can also assist enhance the sales planning process in several ways, including AI-based insights and predictive intelligence[3]. It can positively impact your team's morale by increasing job satisfaction[3].

Marketing and sales are the areas of business operations where it is widely predicted that AI will drive enormous change[4]. In fact, a McKinsey study found that along with other areas of business operations, AI could potentially automate up to 45% of tasks currently performed by humans in marketing[4].

Companies that reach out to a new lead within an hour are seven times likelier to have a successful conversation with decision-makers. Instead of spending 15 to 30 minutes on the phone with one lead, salespeople can scale their speed by responding to multiple prospects simultaneously through AI and text messaging.

Texting is now a preferred sales communication tool combined with AI. In North America, the average text is opened in under five minutes with a 98% open rate; e-mail has an open rate less than 20%.

Seven years ago, I was advising a company, Zipwhip, now Twilio. We had text-enabled all phones at a large luxury car dealership in Seattle. One of the first in the industry. In the first week a service advisor was scheduling a service appointment with an executive by text. He mentioned the new model was in with some features the executive may like. There was some interest, so the salesperson at the dealership texted the executive. From there, the entire transaction was done by text, documents signed etc. The customer came into the dealership, dropped off the old car and picked up the new car. A $90,000 transaction, all digital, with no face-to-face interaction.

Brian Michels, Sales Leader from Tacoma Dodge stated that a significant portion of transactions-over 50%-occur outside of the dealership floor. People buy without meeting face to face. Michels also stated that five years ago a car buyer visited five car dealerships before purchasing a vehicle. Today 1.4 dealerships are being visited on average before buying.

How about most people's largest purchase?

National Association of Realtors (NAR) estimates that home buyers tour at least eight homes before making an offer[2].

This includes both virtual tours and live tours[3]. However, because of how much information is available online, some homebuyers may only tour one home in person before making an offer[3].

A report by <u>domino</u> states that buyers view an average of <u>nine homes</u>[4].

The actual number of homes toured varies based on the market, how busy it is, and how many homes are for sale[2]. Estimates are over 30 homes toured in person 20 years ago before a purchase.

Purchase intention data is another latest silver bullet and is mind-blowing data.

Four friends and relatives in the last two years have purchased Tesla's all without setting foot in the dealership.

Texting in my opinion, as a business tool, is also a nascent technology and will go hand in glove with the rise in technology.

Let's dig into the specifics of how sales teams can use business texting to solve common sales problems.

1. Respond to leads faster

Prospects look at multiple companies when considering a solution, so sales teams can stand out amongst their competitors by being the first to respond to a lead. Research shows that companies that reach out to a new lead within an hour are **seven times likelier** to have a successful conversation with decision-makers than those who respond even 60 minutes later.

Instead of spending 15 to 30 minutes on the phone with one lead, salespeople can scale their speed by responding to multiple prospects simultaneously through text messaging. Some customers may automate the process to generate a message to any new lead that comes in. Sales teams can book appointments over text, too, and later use it to send appointment reminders to reduce no-shows.

Trayco's Air Purifiers

Peter from Trayco's Air Purifiers here. We got your inquiry about purchasing multiple units for your office building. Would you be available to speak this week?

Hi, Peter. Thanks for the quick follow-up! I'm free tomorrow at noon CT if that slot works for you.

That works great! Could I get your full name and email, please?

An air purifier company reaches out to a new lead quickly.

2. Qualify leads faster

Speaking to unqualified leads is a massive waste for sales teams, considering the average sales cycle can last anywhere from three to nine months. Time spent on unqualified leads takes the attention away from higher-quality leads, who can slip through the cracks if not prioritized. The earlier sales teams can qualify a lead, the easier it is for them to decide where to invest their efforts.

Business texting is an effective way to qualify leads in less time because texting has a high response rate of 45 percent, compared to other channels like email at six percent. Salespeople can also juggle more conversations through text than phone calls because they aren't glued to their phones for hours trying to figure out if a lead is worth the investment.

An HR company qualifies a lead via text.

3. Reduce no-shows

Frequent appointment no-shows can drive-up sales costs, like the cost per acquisition, or CPA, by hundreds of dollars. Sales representatives can text their prospects appointment reminders to keep demos or calls on the calendar in a low-touch manner. A gentle reminder text can decrease the chances of no-shows occurring, as one of the common reasons they occur is forgetfulness.

Pink Mink Marketing

Hey, Patrick, it's Zhang from Pink Mink Marketing. I have you on my calendar for tomorrow at noon CT for a check-in call. Does that time still work for you?

Hey, Zhang. Noon CT works great.

A marketing agency uses text to confirm an appointment to reduce no-shows.

4. Close opportunities quicker

When the time comes to close a deal, sales reps can speed up the process by using texting's back-and-forth nature to nail out any details during the negotiation stage. From there, they can text links to documents to ask for e-signatures, guide prospects to a payment page, or send payment reminders. Texts have a 98 percent open rate, and links in texts have an eight times higher click-through rate than other marketing channels, ensuring that buyers will see the messages and know what action to take.

> **Capybara HR**
>
> Hey, Nida, here's a link to the contract I walked you through in today's call. We need a few e-signatures from you to move forward. Let me know if you have any questions. https://bit.ly/6yNtKH3n.
>
> Thanks for sending that over!

A salesperson sends a link to get an e-signature from a new client.

5. Stay in touch for reselling opportunities

Customer retention is a top revenue-driver and is considerably cheaper than customer acquisition efforts. According to Temkin Group, loyal customers are five times likelier to repurchase and seven times likelier to try a new offering. Texting keeps customers in close contact, so salespeople don't have to sweat about missing out on a resell opportunity due to poor timing. Salespeople can proactively reach out to customers to anticipate their needs to increase resell or upsell opportunities to drive the lifetime value, or LTV, of a customer.

RH Data Solutions

Hi, Anastasia. I've noticed you've needed to purchase more seats for our software over the past few months. I ran the numbers, and you would save a lot more money if you upgraded to our Premiere plan. Are you available for a call this week to talk?

Hey, Gary! Thanks for reaching out. We've been growing rapidly, and I meant to ask you about upgrading our plan, but it kept slipping my mind. I'm free Wednesday or Friday from 9 to noon. Let me know what time works for you.

A salesperson uses text for an upsell opportunity.

When I began my sales career, I was making a hundred + calls a day I would speak with someone, then set up an in-person meeting and begin to sort out if the opportunity is qualified.

There are several ways to determine if someone on your website intends to purchase your product or service. One of the best indicators of purchase intent is the kind of content your visitors are consuming. Different types of content are known to draw users at different areas of the buying process. For example, an article titled "How to Do My Small Business Taxes" shows the informational intent of someone who needs tax assistance[1].

Another way is to measure audience purchase intent observationally. You can account for all channels and identify key demographics. You can also understand context within typical paths-to-purchase and ask your users[2].

Finally, you can use decision models to describe sets of logical factors related to the formation of purchase intentions, such as an individual's preexisting disposition to trust, or a website's structural assurances[3].

Learn more:

instapage.com2. instapage.com3. hbr.org4. envision.io5. forbes. com6. hostpapa.com7. hbr.org8. surveymonkey.com9. instapage.com10. instapage.com11. hbr.org12. godaddy.com13. namogoo.com14. godaddy. com15. namogoo.com+11 more

Attention, Revenue generation professionals: our world is changing dramatically, and you haven't seen anything yet; it's going to be a fascinating ride.

Third course will be why is the technology and AI important in your world.

In summary, **today**:

- You can develop massive data on who is interested in your product /solution. Their information is on your website and blogs.

- You can find any prospective customer.

- AI and marketing automation tools will provide personalized outreach.

- AI will develop a targeted prospective customer list.

- AI will set a cadence for communication.

- AI will provide intelligent responses to customers and prospective customers.

- AI will qualify leads.

- AI will close opportunities.

- AI will send agreements and receive agreements.

Are the golden days of selling gone?

Salespeople are still necessary today because they create the interpersonal relationships that inspire prospects to become customers[1]. It is difficult for AI to sort out a prospects ERB -Emotional Reason for Buying. We also know that 90% of communication is non-verbal, a skill only humans possess. The role of a sales professional in today's workplace is complex. A successful salesperson needs to master both hard and soft skills to achieve their professional goals[2]. The modern salesperson does so much more than just close sales. Success in today's sales environment is all about having a transparent strategy and strong presentation to gain your client's trust. It's about building ongoing relationships, doing your research, and personalizing the client experience based on the data you have[3].

The tools, people and other resources required for success include salesperson tools that leverage technology to make the work of sales professionals easier. These applications and software help salespeople identify prospective leads and create personalized conversations for these leads. They increase sales velocity, save time on tedious administrative tasks, and shorten the sales cycle[7].

Learn more:

hoffeldgroup.com2. betterup.com3. forbes.com4. saleshacker.com5. salesforce.com6. salesforce.com7. indeed.com8. salesforce.com9. blog.

hubspot.com10. bing.com11. open.lib.umn.edu12. forbes.com13. indeed.com14. blog.hubspot.com

Here's a story that might help you understand how to communicate with prospective customers when you have data about them and do not want to appear creepy.

There was a company that had a lot of data about its customers. They knew what their customers liked, what they didn't like, and what they were interested in. They wanted to use this data to communicate with their customers in a way that was helpful and not creepy.

So, they decided to use the data to personalize their communication with their customers. They would send emails and messages that were tailored to each customer's interests and needs. For example, if a customer had recently purchased a product, they would send them an email with tips on how to use the product or how to get the most out of it.

They also made sure to be transparent about how they were using the data. They let their customers know that they were using the data to provide a better experience and that they were not sharing the data with anyone else.

By using the data to personalize their communication and being transparent about how they were using it, the company was able to communicate with their customers in a way that was helpful and not disturbing. They were able to build trust with their customers and create a better experience for everyone."

Leveraging technology and a proven sales methodology means less friction with prospects; more revenue and more time for you.

Fourth course: what your work and life will look like

"In the year 2050, AI has become an integral part of human life; it's not referred to as AI. It has revolutionized every aspect of human life from healthcare to education and entertainment. AI has made it possible for humans to live longer and healthier lives by providing personalized healthcare services that are tailored to everyone's needs[1]. It has also transformed education by providing personalized learning experiences that cater to each student's unique learning style[1].

AI has diagnosed and prescribed a course to mitigate pollution and climate change .

AI has also made it possible for humans to explore space in ways that were previously impossible. With AI-powered spacecraft, humans can now travel farther into space than ever before[2].

However, with all these advancements come new challenges. As AI becomes more advanced, it becomes increasingly difficult for humans to understand how it works[3]. This could lead to a situation where humans become overly reliant on AI and lose their ability to think critically[3].

Despite these challenges, AI has the potential to change humankind for the better by making our lives easier and more fulfilling[4].

Artificial Intelligence (AI) is different from previous technologies in several ways. AI has been working incessantly in reducing the risk factor associated with completing a task as compared to other technologies[1]. Unlike other forms of technology or human intelligence for that matter, AI works so efficiently that it leaves no chance for errors or mistakes[1]. AI sensors to forecast and measure the intensity of an earthquake beat the normal scales to measure the earthquakes.

[1]. Forecasts or predictions made by AI are far more accurate than those made by preceding technologies[1].

The key that makes AI different from most other technologies is its strong research background[2]. By default, the computer science field has been an open community marked by academic conferences[2]. Transformative AI initiatives can change how businesses run, shape, and grow uncovering new possibilities, and making AI different from other technologies enabling digital transformation[3].

AI has been making significant strides in recent years and will continue to do so in the future. According to Forbes, here are ten major predictions that will have a broad impact on the way we conduct education, business, healthcare, and many other aspects of our lives over the next decade and beyond[1]:

- AI will become more human-like.
- AI will become more specialized.
- AI will become more autonomous.
- AI will become more explainable.
- AI will become more secure.
- AI will become more ubiquitous.
- AI will become more personalized.
- AI will become more eco-friendly.
- AI will become more ethical.
- AI will become more regulated.

As for how it will impact our lives, experts say that the rise of artificial intelligence will make most people better off over the next decade[2]. However, many have concerns about how advances in AI will affect what it means to be human, to be productive and to exercise free will[2]."

"AI will help keep senior residents social and healthy and will keep family members up-to-date and informed on the care that they are receiving. This can lead to increases in family satisfaction, positive word of mouth, higher occupancy, and increased revenue for senior care facilities." [1]

Another way AI can help senior citizens is by predicting and preventing falls. AI devices that can predict and prevent falls are evolving. This may give seniors with conditions such as Parkinson's Disease the confidence to leave the house, rather than have the fear of falling keeps them prisoner at home[2].

AI is also helping anti-aging researchers understand the very process of aging and thereby develop methods to delay the process. Calico uses deep learning to understand the fundamental biology of aging. Insilico Medicine is a drug development company that uses AI to explore ways to end aging and age-related diseases [3]."

Fifth course: what is the timeframe for these changes?

Now- it's happening and subscribe to the newsletter to stay current on updates.

Sixth course: dessert -a roadmap.

To develop a roadmap; you must know where you are and where you want to go. The challenge is we don't have a 100% clear windshield on how the technologies are developing. The technologies are changing rapidly, and your company is unique in its value proposition and product/solution. The newsletters will provide window cleaner to provide the latest updates.

Our group provides a simple audit and roadmap tailored to your organization.

Deliverables are:

Current State of your business for revenue generation

Desired future state of revenue generation

The gaps between your current and future state.

The initiatives that will take you to your future state.

A plan that recommends:

Technology

People

Organization Structure

Process changes

A roadmap with initiatives prioritized and timeframes.

What does this mean for revenue generation?

1-There is an abundance of online information.

2-Consumers utilize online resources for education about purchases.

3-Consumers will purchase online so there is less need for human intervention…large purchases such as automobile and houses has changed dramatically and requires less and less human interaction. More on this later…

4-Sales professionals can gather incredible data about an individual buyer and company and the reasons and strategic initiatives about why a company will buy a product or services.

5-What and who a prospective company is looking at specifically.

6-Where a prospective client is within the buying pipeline

Sales is no longer all relationship selling the shift is to more technology selling and data driven sales.

The world has changed and will continue to change.

Postscript-Quantum Computing, if you are interested.

Quantum computing is a relatively new type of computer programming that incorporates quantum mechanics into a machine's functionality. It may result in faster computer processing, especially when working with large data sets[1]. Quantum computing is expected to revolutionize the tech industry by enabling faster and more efficient computing[2].

Here's a short story about quantum computing:

"Once upon a time, there was a scientist named Alice who was working on a project that required her to process large amounts of data. She had been using traditional computers for years and found that they were too slow for her needs. One day, she heard about quantum computing and decided to give it a try.

Alice was amazed at how fast quantum computers could process data. She was able to complete her project in record time and was even able to discover new insights that she wouldn't have been able to find with traditional computers.

From that day on, Alice became a big advocate for quantum computing and encouraged others to try it out for themselves."

Chapter 11

Channel Management

Did you know Forrester claims 75% of all revenue is through reseller partners, a dramatic and drastic change from 2013 when sales were primarily direct sales? And the time we last published our book. Hence, the reason for the update. Enjoy!

How can you leverage your time/effort and maximize revenue through channel sales?

For inspiration, look no further than a company named Databox. Their CEO and former HubSpot VP of Sales Pete Caputa describes what happened when HubSpot was preparing to launch a partner program: "From day one, we started hosting a lot of educational webinars. … When they were over, I just sat back and watched the interest in our program fly in." Hubspot was able to identify their key personas, give them content that was relevant, and successfully find more channel partners.

In my opinion, Pete forgot some of the hard work it took to develop the launch and the training and follow-up with partners.

HubSpot found that the LTV:CAC* (Lifetime Value of a customer: Customer Acquisition Cost) ratio when selling directly was 1.5, while the same rate was as much as 5 when selling through the channel.

I have developed over 40 channel partnerships, lots of learning/scar tissue. Below is a definition of channel partnerships, how to recruit/select partners, compensation, onboarding, and optimization of partners. Your playbook for channel partnerships is below.

Definition of channel sales

Channel sales — or selling through partners — represents 75% of the world's commerce, according to Forrester. This approach helps companies accelerate sales and grow revenue without adding to their headcount, a move that's increasingly important during economic uncertainty.

Whether you're launching a channel to scale more efficiently, tap into new markets, or meet customer needs, this chapter will assist you in it; you'll learn the basics of channel sales and how it can work for you. For those already well versed in working with partners, feel free to skip ahead to the sections most helpful to you.

In channel sales, companies sell through intermediaries. These intermediaries go by many names in different contexts: partners, resellers, dealers, distributors, brokers, agents, affiliates — the list goes on. This business model is also called indirect selling because the company doesn't have a direct connection to the end customer.

Indirect or channel sales have also exploded because of technology. A small company may now tap into the resources of a behemoth with established buyers, communications, and channels of distribution. It requires a solid approach and disciplined approach. The approach is the same, but here are some different tools, and this will also be covered later in this book.

Channel sales is a way to boost revenue from existing products by getting them in front of previously unreached consumers. Estimates are that it has grown 50% in less than ten years.

There are several ways to maximize revenues through channel sales partners. Here are some high-level tips to consider; a more extensive checklist will be provided:

- Look for partners that are a DNA fit. When considering companies that would be ideal to sell your products and services, make sure the fit is logical and, if possible, long-term in nature[1]

- Build relationships with partners. Building a relationship with your channel partners is key to success[1]

- Equip your partners for success Provide your partners with the necessary tools and resources to sell your products and services[1]

- Make sure you can scale along with new channel opportunities[1]

- Promote product education, adjust pricing structures, run discount and sales promotions, or try new marketing tactics[2]

- Automate account mapping, automate pipeline sharing, and auto connect sales reps to co-sell with partners on their mutual accounts[3]

Choose your partners carefully. A solid channel strategy is based on quality not quantity

Learn more:

1. entrepreneur.com2. incentivesolutions.com3. blog.hubspot.com4. accenture.com5. saleshacker.com6. blog.zoovu.com+3 more

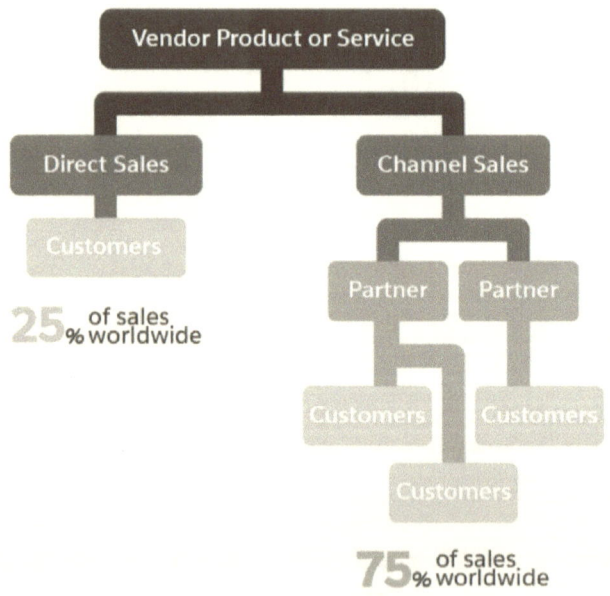

While indirect sales use a go-between, direct selling does not. Under a direct sales model, the brand sells straight to the end consumer. For instance, a brand might sell through its own retail store or its own website.

Many companies use a mix of direct and indirect sales. They may have customers who prefer buying through a channel (for example, a third-party retail store), while other customers might prefer buying from the manufacturer. Below are a few examples to help illustrate this point.

Direct sales: Sales where the company sells directly to the end customer.

Indirect sales: Sales that use an intermediary such as partners, resellers, dealers, or brokers. Also called channel sales.

Who do you need to make it happen?

Channel sales managers are expected, by their organizations, and their partners, to perform at the highest professional standards across a wide range of **sales** disciplines. They are expected to train and coach a sales team they had no role or responsibility in hiring. Some have said this is one of the most skilled positions on a revenue generation team.

Here are some examples of channel sales strategies [3]:

- Stepping out of existing distribution channels to embrace a new selling strategy is a way to boost revenue from existing products by getting them in front of previously unreached consumers.

- Selling via retailers, distributors, e-commerce sites, direct mail, and wholesalers encompasses a wide array of potential channels where consumers can shop.

- The goal of each channel strategy can vary, depending on a company's overarching marketing and sales objectives. For example, a new company may want to create a channel strategy focused on generating brand awareness, while a well-established company might focus more on expanding into an untapped market.

Pros and cons of channel sales

Pros:

Easier Scaling

Scaling a business is one of the biggest challenges owners faces. There's a limit to how much you can optimize current lead generation approaches, and expanding into new markets takes a lot of planning and resources.

With the assist of channel sales, you can avoid many of the challenges that go with scaling your business, shifting the large portion of the work to third-party partners who will generate sales for you.

If you find the right partners, you can gain instant access to large markets you had no way of reaching before, which can accelerate growth and ensure that the flow of new business doesn't run out.

What's more, channel sales also assist you leverage the human resources your partners can offer. There are only so many salespeople you have at your disposal, and at some point, the rate at which you can convert leads into clients is going to stagnate.

However, if you partner up with another business that sells for you, that means you can focus on running your business after getting your partners up to speed, then some less labor-intensive monitoring, if done correctly. Then, you start thinking about the fact that you can potentially partner up with dozens of companies, and the potential for scaling becomes almost limitless.

Reaching New Customers

Reaching new audiences is a big challenge. For one thing, you are limited in how many channels you can pursue at once. And at the same time, you might not have the budget or the experience to tackle some of the approaches your competitors are using.

That's where channel sales can come in as a massive boost to your efforts of expanding.

If you can develop strategic partnerships with companies that are able to enter a particular market, you can cut through a lot of the obstacles you would face on your own and start generating sales much faster.

This way, you can take advantage of the expertise and know-how of the company you're partnering with, avoiding the costs of having to figure everything out on your own and taking advantage of the unique position you can find yourself in.

For instance, if you want to sell your product in a different country, you can probably imagine how much red tape and issues you would have to overcome before making a single sale. Meanwhile, if you find the right sales channel that works locally, you can avoid that altogether and get straight to generating sales without having to worry about any of the details.

Reduced Costs

One of the top priorities for any business is to maximize the lifetime value of a customer while also minimizing the cost of acquiring them. To achieve that, a company must be willing to continually track and tweak its approach, prioritizing areas with the biggest returns over those that take up time without producing the desired outcomes.

And even though channel sales do have some costs associated with compensating the third-party providing the sale, it might still turn out to be the most profitable and cost-effective way of generating **enterprise sales** and growing your business.

Sure, you probably have reliable and tested direct sales approaches that have worked for a long time and are generating good results. And at the same time, you will only find out whether channel sales could do even better if you give it a try and expand your network.

For instance, **HubSpot found** that the LTV:CAC* (Lifetime Value of a customer: Customer Acquisition Cost) ratio when selling directly was 1.5, while the same rate was as much as 5 when selling through the channel.

The difference might not be as stark in your case, but it's always good to try and expand your ability to make sales through multiple channels and then see which ones are the most profitable.

*Lifetime Value: Customer Acquisition Cost

Built-In Trust

Entering a new market is not easy. Especially if you're a startup or a less-known company that isn't yet known in that region. Luckily, there's a way to circumvent that issue entirely by leveraging the authority and trust of a partner you use as a sales channel.

When you use a sales channel that has a strong reputation in a specific market, you can make the sales much easier and reduce friction by leveraging that reputation to your advantage.

Instead of having to build trust from the ground up using brand awareness campaigns, you can leave the process to someone who has in-depth knowledge of how that market operates, what approaches work best, and how to use their previous success to sell your products faster and with better margins.

Other channel partner benefits:

- Bigger network. Partners can introduce your brand to customers who are not in your existing circles and help you scale up sales faster than you could on your own.

- Amplified reach. Partners can magnify your marketing efforts with their own by hosting local events, driving webinar registrations, or providing onsite training with customers.

- Lower overhead. Indirect selling doesn't involve a lot of the expenses you'd incur from direct selling, such as employee salaries, health insurance, office space, and mileage, because partners are not your employees.

- Customer satisfaction. Partnerships can round out your solution with complementary products or services. If your customers prefer to buy one complete experience, indirect selling allows you to better serve how they want to be served.

- Approved vendor . A partner may be an approved vendor in complex purchasing scenarios and you may utilize their privileged position

Cons

Even though the advantages of using channel sales are substantial, it does have some drawbacks as well. Let's look at them below:

Having to Share Revenue

The most obvious disadvantage of channel sales is having to share your profits with a third party. When you generate sales on your own, you get to keep all the profits minus the customer acquisition cost, but with channel sales, additional expenses will also have to be paid depending on the type of arrangement you've reached.

However, this is not really that big of an issue if you manage to find the right partner.

For one thing, if a partner can offer you the opportunity to scale and expand, the sheer amount of sales will more than compensate for the percentage you must share.

What's more, they will likely take over parts of the sales process, meaning that acquiring sales costs less for you as well.

Finally, every sale you make is an opportunity for more sales down the line to the same customer. If you can ensure a high customer lifetime value, you can be very generous with your channel sales partners and still make a hefty profit.

Keep in mind this is incremental revenue for your organization.

Less Control Over Your Brand

Protecting your brand's reputation is a top priority. And while you can control how your sales team interacts with customers, you won't have the same control when you use channel sales and partnerships with other companies.

That will be a compromise you will have to make when you decide to expand through channel sales, which might not be something all business owners are willing to do.

However, the good news is that even though it's impossible to have the same control as you would with direct sales, you can still establish rules and processes that offer at least some protections. With these in place, you can set up guidelines for how the opportunities must be set up and give yourself more control over the sales timeline, ensuring more predictable revenue.

Finding Reliable Partners Can Be Difficult

When using channel sales, managing partners is a hassle that you'll have to get used to. Not all partners are created equal, and some might underperform or turn out to be unreliable.

And unfortunately, there's not much you can do about that, at least initially. Before you gain more experience with channel sales, knowing who's a good fit will mostly be a guessing game. You will also need time to develop processes and guidelines that work in your industry and situation.

The good news is that just as with any other marketing or sales approach, time and testing usually solve most of these problems. And as you collect more data, you can weed out the partners not generating the necessary results and learn what to look for based on the ones that are performing well.

Fewer Customer Insights

For a business, one of the biggest advantages of making direct sales is the number of insights you can gain about your customers.

Since your sales team won't get to have direct conversations with prospects, you will miss out on some of the data you could have had when qualifying a lead over the phone, email or text which can seem limiting.

Potential conflicts

When you use a hybrid of direct and indirect selling, sometimes your partners may feel like they're competing with your own salespeople. Creating clear guidelines around what products are sold through the channel versus direct sales will minimize this issue.

However, in many cases, you will find that the sales you generate through your partners were from markets you didn't have access to, which means you wouldn't have had access to the insights from those sales in the first place.

And as you work with the customers after the sale, there will still be plenty of opportunities to learn more about them and figure out how to cater to your audience's needs more effectively.

Where to begin?

Develop a channel sales strategy.

Your channel strategy should align to your company's overall sales strategy. Start by defining your program's purpose. This could be a mission statement that outlines what the program offers to partners and what you will do for them and with them. For example, you might say:

"Our partner program is designed to offer resellers and distributors the support and solution expertise they need at every step. We aim to provide our diverse partner network with the tools, technology, and personalized resources they rely on to better serve their customers, build loyalty, and accelerate revenue growth."

You can display this statement on the public landing page of your partner portal so that potential partners understand what you're all about. This statement should also guide decisions as the program grows.

Next, define goals for your channel sales program and consider the following:

- Set realistic joint expectations between direct and indirect sales teams.

- Outline sales and co-marketing activities and expected pipeline results with partners.

- Define target market and product/solution offerings.

- Create rules of engagement, especially if the partners sell competitors' products, too.

- Establish key performance indicators to track progress.

- Spend time in vetting, qualifying, and understanding partners. The wrong partners will consume valuable time and resources. Focus on quality over quantity, stressing sales growth, and innovation.

Well-defined goals propel channel sales, create better partner alignment, and ensure a flourishing relationship between vendors and partners.

If your policies and guidelines create confusion or leave room for interpretation, that can create problems. Make sure these documents are as clear and thorough as possible.

Get to know their business goals. How will you support their business objectives?

Develop comprehensive training programs so that partners know your products inside and out. Always be ready to answer their questions.

Bottom Line

A channel sales strategy can be one of the most powerful ways to accelerate the growth of your business and expand into markets you couldn't otherwise reach.

If you are willing to accept the potential drawbacks and take the time to carefully recruit and select your partners, onboard them and monitor and evaluate progress, there's no reason why channel sales could not become your most powerful strategy for generating sales.

All employees need tools and resources to complete their job. And to be successful in the job, the tools and resources should be engaging and inspirational. Use internal company content to resonate with channel partners so that they can be inspired to drive higher sales. It is imperative early on to show the partner sales team how to sell your solution and have a shared sales prospect pipeline. Channel partner marketing is just as important when attracting channel partners as it is for retaining them.

Types of Channel Sales Partnerships

At this point, you maybe convinced that the advantages channel sales can offer considerably outweigh the risks and challenges it can come with. And to make the most of what it has to offer, it's also essential to understand the **types of sales partnerships** you can potentially use. Your support and partner compensation needs to be structured depending on the type of partnership.

Let's look at them below:

- Referral Partners. One of the most common types of channel sales partnerships is a referral partner. They could be business partners or even clients you trust, who refer qualified leads to you in exchange for a commission.

- Retailers. If you have physical products with a more general demand, you could utilize retailers in physical shops or showrooms to get your product in front of more people.

- Outsourced sales. Sometimes, you might decide to outsource an entire sales team that would source and close clients for you.

- White label. You could also allow your channel sales partners to add their branding to your product, limiting your brand's exposure and reducing some of the risks associated with this method.

- Installation. You may not have a global installation network and your product/services require installation.

- Investment /take-out — a trial relationship, may be a value-added reseller, or referral/sales partner where their company will benefit from owning your company.

- Affiliates. Affiliates are websites that get paid a commission to send customers to a merchant's website. A makeup brand might use beauty bloggers or social influencers as affiliates to promote its lip gloss and bronzers online.

- Alliances. Alliances are partnerships with companies that sell complementary products. For instance, a cloud software company might provide enterprise storage in partnership with another tech company.

- Dealers. Dealers serve as an intermediary between customers and the manufacturer. Car manufacturers sell except Tesla through dealerships.

- Distributors. Distributors buy directly from the businesses, then market and sell to customers in their operating regions. For instance, a beverage manufacturer sells directly to distributors, who then sell those products to stores and restaurants in a specific geographic area.

- Franchisees. Franchisees pay to use a brand's identity, processes, and business model to sell that brand's products or services. Some gyms license their brand to independently owned and operated franchise locations.

- Resellers or VARs. Resellers or value-added resellers (VARs) purchase existing products with the intention of reselling them, often adding features or services to enhance value. Many software companies sell through resellers or VARs.

Recruiting and selecting channel partners

1. DEFINE YOUR CHANNEL PARTNER PROGRAM BEFORE STARTING RECRUITING

A strong product won't be enough to persuade other companies to promote it on your behalf. You need to have a comprehensive channel program and strategies on how to convey its unique selling points to newly found prospective partners. Collaborate with your internal marketing team to finesse promotional messaging, particularly on your company's webpage.

What's more, you need to anticipate candidates' questions and have answers ready? Make sure you can confidently address:

- What is your commission structure?

- Does your partner program offer growth opportunities for greater revenue share?

- Are there additional perks partners can expect outside of revenue?

- What does the onboarding process look like?

- What is the estimated time commitment you expect from program participants, especially regarding onboarding?

- In what ways can you help promote your partners, and is that available to everyone or a select group?

Most organizations have a "pyramid of partnerships" that reflects their relationship with multiple channel partners. Typically, this pyramid will segment partners according to either or both of the following criteria:

- The amount of money that the partner creates for the organization.

- The loyalty of the partner, as evidenced by the amount of training and certification that the partner has "bought" from the organization.

The problem with this kind of segmentation is that it completely misses out on one of the most important factors in channel performance management — relationship quality.

Research over the last 15 years by Alliance Best Practice has shown that relationship quality is the pre-eminent factor in predicting channel partner success. In short — the better the relationship, the better the results. "Better" in this context means relationship effectiveness and efficiency.

To succeed it's important to do the right things at the right levels to develop the relationship type that you are looking for (effectiveness), and you need to do things right to succeed (efficiency).

Let's illustrate what we mean by comparing a typical segmentation pyramid with a relationship segmentation pyramid.

Two Types of Segmentation Pyramid

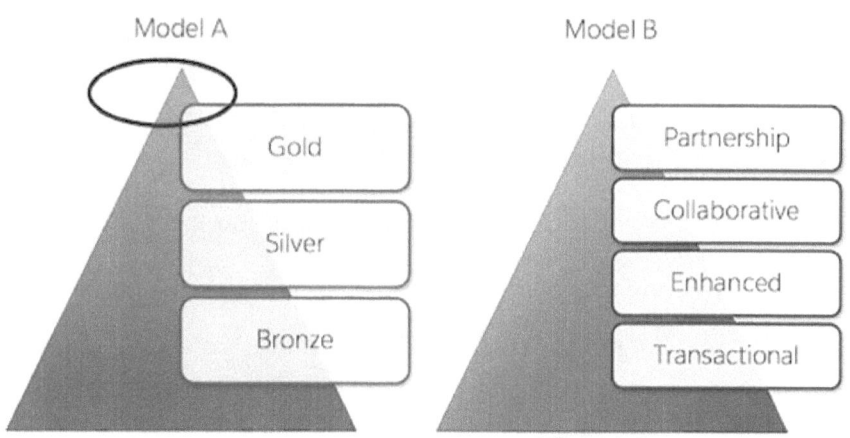

Model A organizes partners by level of engagement, which is defined by the volume of sales and amount of training each partner achieves.

Model B organizes partners by the kind of relationship they have with the host company. The partners are organized as follows:

Stage 4 — Transactional: This is a "buy from" and "sell to" relationship. One partner has an attractive product or service, and the other partner wants to buy it from them and resell it as part of their offerings (sometimes called a reseller model). Business intimacy is low, and the degree of effort dedicated to this relationship should be low as well.

Stage 3 — Enhanced: One partner recognizes it can generate more profit and client/customer interest by "enhancing" the base product or service from the other partner. Enhancement can come in the form of key account knowledge, particular industry sector knowledge, using software accelerators, and so on. This type of relationship is sometimes called a value-added reseller (VAR).

Stage 2 — Collaborative: If two partners have collaborated successfully on a particular product or service, they may conclude that working together in the future would be efficient and profitable. Consequently, they would create a collaborative relationship with an accompanying strategy, governance framework, and geographic scope focus. This is sometimes called "partnering on purpose."

Stage 1 — Partnership: The highest level of inter-organizational collaboration is a partnership. At this stage, both partners work together to develop common and joint business opportunities in areas that are new to both companies. The level of interaction, trust, communication, knowledge exchange, and interoperation are very high. This is sometimes called "shared risk and shared reward" relationships.

This is referred to as the TECP model of inter-business collaboration.

There are fundamental differences between both models.

Lessons from the TECP model include:

• Matching the level to the intent of the relationship is critical to avoid wasting resources.

• The higher up the pyramid, the greater the effort and commitment needed from both partners, but the greater the rewards.

• It is the relationship, rather than the technology, that is the key determinant of alliance success.

• It is important to know where the relationship is starting from. What kind of relationship would be the best fit? Not every external relationship will be a full-blown partnership. The pyramid is the shape it is for a reason. There will be more transactional relationships than enhanced, and more enhanced than collaborative. Partnerships are the rarest relationships of all. This is because both parties must commit increasing amounts of time, loyalty, and resources to reach each new stage. Such commitment is not easily replicated many times even in the largest organization.

• Organizations that don't pay enough attention to growing key partners through the TECP value chain have organizational pyramids that are too flat and overly focused on many partners that are transactional, low margin, or disloyal.

Transactional partners gain the most active focus from salespeople in organizations because they are constantly involved in unearthing or developing tactical opportunities. This doesn't help in developing a "deeper" relationship.

To further elevate your partner recruitment strategy, prepare materials that acknowledge these points.

If you remain ambiguous about any of the above, you're simply not ready to actively find and recruit new channel partners. After all, you only have one opportunity to make a first impression!

2. DON'T FOCUS YOUR RECRUITMENT MESSAGING EXCLUSIVELY ON THE MONEY

Business is business. However, you can't underestimate the human element that underlines many financial decisions. Present your brand as friendly, creative, open-minded, trustworthy, and respectful. Ideally, partners should be excited to collaborate with your team and form a working relationship.

There are numerous ways you can convey this throughout your partner recruitment conversations and content. Perhaps emphasize regular one-on-one communication in which you ask for feedback and share performance reports. Or why not discuss opportunities to co-market joint initiatives offered to high achievers? A quality Partner Relationship Management Software (PRM) expresses elevated sophistication that will prove attractive to partners.

3. IDENTIFY AND CATER TO YOUR POTENTIAL PARTNERS

To find the best channel partners, you need to implement the fundamentals of inbound marketing. Ask yourself who your ideal partner is and develop a persona—a fictional, generalized character that represents the various needs, goals, and behavior patterns among your real and potential partners.

By creating a persona for your ideal partner, you can begin to craft relevant, useful content such as blog posts, white papers, press releases, and newsletters. It helps to be able to ask yourself "Would VP of Marketing, Sally care about this content? Would this content assist her be more efficient in her current role?" By identifying which content types and topics are relevant to your persona, you can easily begin pulling potential partners into the funnel and understanding which partners are a good fit. 96 percent of B2B buyers want content from industry thought leaders, so building a robust, diverse content library can position your company as an industry expert and assist you to recruit the partners best positioned to connect with prospective customers.

4. KNOW YOUR PARTNERS' TARGET CUSTOMERS

Even channel partners with the most potential might not be the right fit if your product doesn't appeal to their core customer base. Newly recruited channel partners need to know that working with your company will establish a mutually beneficial and profitable relationship, which means you need to know who their customers are and whether a partnership makes sense. Otherwise, marketing to their business connections will be next to impossible.

5. BUILD YOUR PRESENCE ON PUBLICATIONS AND CHANNELS WITH WHICH YOUR IDEAL PARTNERS REGULARLY INTERACT

Prior to this step, you laid the groundwork for your program and crafted messaging designed to address candidates' main priorities. Now is the time to shine a spotlight on your brand and channel offering!

Identify which social media channels your ideal partners are likely to utilize and nurture a presence through regular engagement. This strategy doesn't only pertain to your company's social profiles, but your leadership's as well. The goal is to start dialogues, build perceived authority, and slowly cultivate relationships. Don't make the mistake of using social media solely to promote yourself and your channel program.

Take your promotion one step further by considering what publications your ideal candidates trust. Guest podcasting or contributing an article to strategically chosen outlets can significantly boost brand awareness amongst targeted decision-makers.

Like the above, don't shy away from establishing an industry presence through networking. Whether you are the star speaker at an event, operate a booth at a conference, or shake hands at a happy hour, each interaction puts a memorable face to a company name.

Your efforts to foster Industry connections should lead to more prospective partners finding you rather than vice versa. Plus, when you do want to advertise your partner program, candidates should be much more receptive to your recruitment efforts.

6. CREATE "FOMO" BY PROMOTING EXISTING PARTNERS AND CASE STUDIES

We've all heard the phrase "show, don't tell." Take this idiom to heart by promoting partners on your website, co-branding joint materials, and celebrating their successes on social media. Most importantly? Case studies!

Such strategies bring attention to your channel and demonstrate to others the types of rewards that they could enjoy. Additionally, they keep current partners engaged.

KNOW WHEN TO SAY NO TO PROSPECTIVE PARTNERS

Just because an interested company finds your partnership program doesn't mean you should immediately enroll them. Participants that are poorly suited for your brand, products, or audience will ultimately lead to wasted time and resources for everyone involved. Worse, they can misrepresent your company and discourage possible customers.

* Negotiating the partnership

- Look beyond the individual negotiator and consider the counter-party's fundamental interests in the relationship.

- Ask "Why?" to open dialogue.

- Identify ways to create options to resolve disagreements.

    Here are the detailed checklists:

Recruiting and selecting partner companies

Define a business strategy and let it be known.

Develop a marketing plan that includes a defined partner program and portal for partners.

Mindshare= Market Share-how can you obtain the Mindshare?

Performance =Motivation x Learning. How and why is the channel sales team motivated and do they know how to find and close buyers for your solution.

Before you go too far, have a verbal understanding of your company's value to the partner, in their own words.

Who is first, customer or channel partner? Important to understand and prioritize.

How to find and hire the ideal channel manager. We have a testing tool that can be utilized. **Channel sales managers** are expected, by their organizations, and their partners, to perform at the highest professional standards across a wide range of **sales** disciplines. They are expected to train and coach a sales team they had no role or responsibility in hiring. Some have said this is one of the most skilled positions on a revenue generation team.

How to differentiate your channel approach from your competitors, your channel value proposition.

Goldilocks-remember Quality vs Quantity the right # of partners. How many are required to accomplish your revenue objectives vs. bandwidth of your team to support partners.

Recruiting agency within your company. Are there leads for partners from your employees?

Passive companies on linked in or social media that are interested in your company.

Why are organizations buying their product?

How many sales from channel partner will be dedicated to your company?

Why is your company valuable, in their words?

Do you have a way to rank and sort partners, weighted. I suggest a matrix, greater or lesser than average market share in the partner category, as an example.

Agreed upon objectives/goals with stated events and timeframes (e.g., first 90 days and beyond), open office hours, in the trenches working side-by-side, and ongoing training.

Are the partner salespeople open to testing and coaching?

Model different for every company, the and before process . Bring Stated goals and events and timeframes on one line process to engineer the formula is the same.

Coach-ability

Do they understand buyers needs/solutions?

Connectivity with the correct buyers

Learning/development tool (e.g., micro-learning, videos, etc.).

Stated goals by events and

timeframes.

Onboarding channel partners-They are partners-now what?

Without channel partner onboarding and education, untapped revenue quite literally will walk out the door.

* Modeling desired behaviors-teach a person to fish

* Provide a clear, practical guide that will help you design, identify, build, grow and motivate a successful sales-oriented distribution channel.

Here are three reasons why channel partner onboarding strategies are important:

- **Sets partners up for success.** Providing channel partners with the right product knowledge will accelerate successful customer interactions.

- **Ensures across-the-board compliance.** Misalignment on brand guidelines and other compliance-related activities causes a lot of headaches. Proper partner onboarding ensures consistency in branding, compliance, and messaging from the beginning.

- **Activates growth at scale.** When onboarded correctly, channel partners are a surefire way to accelerate company growth. They can articulate your differentiated value proposition, provide real-time support, and get your product into customers' hands faster.

Understanding the channel partner onboarding process

Did you know that channel partners can take **more than a year** to become profitable for your business? This means **time is of the essence** — and so is the need for a productive onboarding strategy.

Let's start with the four main phases of an onboarding process:

- In *discovery*, you and your channel partners collaborate on existing processes and procedures. You gain a better sense of the partner's strengths and weaknesses — and where onboarding can elevate their capabilities to sell your product.

- During *documentation*, you provide your partner with the materials they need to sell to customers. These essential documents can include sell-documents, best practices, marketing assets, and support information.

- Then, you launch *enablement training*, where your channel partners are onboarded to your company, products, brand, and customers. The training also reinforces your value proposition and messaging schemes, so your partner is confident in selling your product over a competitor.

- Finally, *feedback* is the critical stage in which you gather insight used to continuously improve your onboarding program.

Success Factors: Getting your channel partner onboarding strategy right.

When working with the new partner ensure you understand how your value is perceived in the C suite and by each functional leader. Also, what the value of the partnership means to the sales leader and each of the salespeople. Each player will have different motives. The CEO may see that partnership is to increase market value of the company to drive stock price or sell the company, the CFO may see an increased margin opportunity, hence, increasing their compensation and recognition, the CPO (Chief Product Officer) may see an enhanced product offering, bundling your product and increasing their compensation and recognition. The sales leader sees more revenue, increasing their compensation and recognition. The salespeople see more revenue and personal stronger client relations which leads to greater compensation, recognition, and advancement potential.

A warning: ensure you are embedded in the compensation plan for the salespeople. Ideally work toward or be a part of the overall total compensation, not an add-on like an extra 5-10% for the salesperson. Otherwise, you will not receive adequate focus from the leadership team and salespeople.

Finally, keep reinforcing that personal message when you meet, to ensure you get their mindshare, and hence, your revenues. I had a partner, who was an SVP of Sales and Marketing that I worked with. Every year when we renewed our agreement, we would have a dinner at his house and go through projected revenues, and he would show me the impact on his compensation.

Do the math

This may not happen overnight; it is an ideal state. Projecting partner success is gaining commitment and understanding the math to get to your shared goals.

An example:

Your shared revenue goal is $2,000,000.

Average sale is $100,000.

40 sales and you attain your revenue objective.

Average time to close an existing client is 4 months.

Close ratio from interest to close is 20%.

Average time to close a new client is 8 months .

Close ratio from interest to close is 5%.

There are 10 existing clients in the sales pipeline and 10 new clients in the pipeline.

Expected value of the current pipeline $120,000 + $60,000 = $180,000.

The apparent shortfall is $1,820,000

What does that mean?

The math shows how many interested, qualified buyers are needed to generate X number of proposals to attain the $1,820,000 in revenue.

As an example, if the close ratio for proposal is 33%, ~ 18 sales must be closed to attain the revenue target.

Therefore, 55 proposals must be generated to attain 18 sales.

The ratio of qualified buyers in the pipeline that move to proposal is 25%.

So then, 220 new qualified buyers must be added to the pipeline.

This is where you get tactical - getting each salesperson to commit to add more qualified buyers to the pipeline may be easier if they are adding your product to existing clients where there is already a relationship.

To continue the example, say the salespeople commit to add 110 new qualified buyers to the sales pipeline.

Where do the 110 additional qualified buyers come from? We forgot about marketing, and their role in demand generation; that needs to be added. Thanks to Tracy Strudley of Global Ed, New Zealand for the insight and reminder.

Be certain marketing is involved from the beginning and is accountable and responsible for adding qualified buyers to the pipeline and has agreed upon number.

When planning onboarding, you will not be perfect in training, and will learn and iterate as you go. Some planning ideas:

How much training in joint sales calls vs curriculum?

Best way or blend to deliver training – in-person, online, visual, auditory?

You will find clues to how the organization learns in how they communicate.

There are several learning styles:

Visual - learning through watching and seeing. Verbal cues - see, saw.

Auditory - learning through listening and hearing sounds. Verbal cues – hear, heard.

Kinesthetic - learning through physical activity or body movement (this involves the vestibular and proprioceptive senses); Verbal cues - move, physical action oriented words.

Tactile - learning through using the sense to touch. Verbal cues - feel…

Olfactory and Gustatory - learning through smell and taste. Verbal cues, taste, smell…doesn't smell right…

Every organization and person has their own learning style. Here is a roadmap for your onboarding optimization.

Creating a channel partner onboarding strategy can be a bit daunting at first. In fact, you may already be asking yourself any (or all) of these questions:

- Where do we start?

- What information should we include in the channel partner training?

- What are we trying to achieve?

- How can we make this easy for our partners?

These questions are a solid first step! Also, because we've been around the channel partner training block a time or two, here are some of our best practices:

Set goals for the program.

Before embarking on any new training strategy, it's essential to know **what it is you're trying to achieve**. Do you want to better support your partners with more hands-on training? Amplify sales growth? Reduce customer churn?

No matter what your aim is, write them down and remember to check in on your goals along the way.

Conduct a gap analysis.

Different partners face different challenges, which is why it's smart to start your onboarding journey by tapping into their specific needs with a gap analysis. By going directly to the source, you can identify:

- Knowledge gaps

- Inconsistencies

- Common mistakes or misunderstandings

- Product shortcomings

All of which should be addressed in the onboarding information.

Consider the nuances of various partners.

Working with a variety of channel partners means their onboarding experiences might look different from one another. If you partner with a combination of distributors, independent dealers, independent sales agents (ISA), service delivery partners, or others, **consider creating onboarding courses tailored to their needs.**

Identify essential internal stakeholders.

Now, it's time to look internally. Pinpoint internal stakeholders that will play a key role in developing, managing, and distributing the onboarding program.

Likely internal stakeholders to consider are:

- Channel managers

- Technical experts

- Product managers

- Sales trainers

Streamline your training delivery.

Getting your onboarding program into the hands of your partners and joint sales calls; teach a person to fish.

Follow up.

Once your channel partner onboarding program is off the ground, don't take your foot off the gas just yet!

Remember to set 30/60/90-day check-ins to follow up with your channel partners. These check-ins are valuable ways to learn how the programs are or are not helping them understand, message, and sell your product to customers.

Non-cash incentives

Partners will sell other products. Getting their attention quickly is important. I recommend non-cash travel or merchandise incentives to increase the speed of adoption of your product to a new partner. It takes 21 days to establish a habit. This is a proven way to get the partner sales team motivated - ideally tie in a trip to meet with your team and if possible, include the significant other. Extra cash is proven to not be as effective. *See the postscript at the end of the chapter for more details if you are interested.*

Onboarding sales training, methodology and coaching –what does it look like?

* Modeling desired behaviors

*Provide a clear, practical guide that will help you design, identify, build, grow and motivate a successful sales-oriented distribution channel. Including:

Buyer journey.

Sales process.

Qualifying matrix.

Detailed sales training.

Course agenda.

Does training to salespeople include experiencing the day-to-day job of potential customers?

Is social media encouraged/ utilized by salespeople? Understand buyer's goals and how it fits.

Doctor/patient relationship—asking the right questions.

Metrics driven sales coaching.

Coaching plan with the referral partner, salesperson and/or organization.

Understand each salespersons' superpower.

Metrics to diagnose which skill development area that will have the biggest impact on the salesperson's performance.

Strong set of performance exams and certifications, if technical.

How do you measure coaching success, improvement, leads generated, leads worked, demos, and customers.

Set realistic targets.

A part of motivating channel partners is **managing and setting realistic sales goals.** When channel partners are given attainable targets, they are more likely to succeed. Lowering expectations will not only decrease stress on the sales team but with the right motivation, it will push them to set their goals even higher. The tactic of aiming for less will demonstrate to channel partners that they can meet their goals and the success they experience will give them the drive to reach beyond that.

Don't forget to ---Praise Channel Partners

When a channel partner or a channel sales team meets a quota, praise them! Not just when a quota is met, but anytime a goal is achieved or simply because you see a team member who is having a good, productive day. Praising channel partners will make them feel appreciated and valued. It's a feeling that everyone desires. By simply praising and encouraging channel partners, the company will see a boost in results. We all crave recognition; **implementing a reward program** will also help with this.

Incentivize channel partners to increase channel sales.

Sometimes it may take a little **incentive to motivate channel partners** to sell to their full capabilities. An incentive can be something as simple as a friendly competition amongst team members (i.e., top channel sales partner for the month of June will win a $100 pre-paid credit card) or you can build out a full **rewards program**. Rewards programs have been proven to show huge spikes in channel engagement.

Provide channel partners with support and build a relationship.

A well-managed channel partner will bring the company success. Sales teams need to feel like they have support. Channel managers and leaders need to be available to build a relationship with their channel teams and provide the proper support needed. Creating a relationship with channel partners can be of great benefit — be a business friend and reap the benefits of that friendship.

Continually Assess Your Partner Recruitment Funnel To Find Improvements

Not every conversation you have with a prospect will ultimately lead to a new partner. However, even the ones that don't work out will bring value if you learn from them. If a company ultimately declines to join, politely ask for feedback. You may start to discern similarities between different individuals' answers or the point in which they choose to disengage.

Is your revenue share not competitive enough? Are informative materials failing to resonate with the readers? Such insights can go a long way to improving the effectiveness of your partner recruitment tactics.

Spotlight Your Partner Relationship Management As Part Of Your Partner Recruitment Conversations

Partners naturally seek assurance of smooth operations, battle-tested strategies, and your overall dedication to their success. After all, a partner program that runs like a well-oiled machine fueled by new sales content and marketing will make it easier for them to sell products.

Set up recently recruited candidates with their own **prospect pages** within your PRM so they can witness first-hand the enticing new customer experience. Share with them a sneak peek of your **content library** in which they can view its robustness and ease of use.

Your willingness to invest in technology demonstrates professionalism and commitment to their long-term success.

Dedicate Times Towards A Well-Designed Partner Page

Don't de-value your partner page, as this is content all prospects will read sooner or later. Make sure your messaging is purposeful, the design is polished, and that you give readers compelling reasons to further engage.

Optimizing channel partners-ongoing relationship

Sales compensation/incentives

What types of current sales compensation plans are in place?

What is being paid to the salespeople ?

Are they being paid a % of revenue ?

Where quota attainment and accelerators are for exceeding quota, is your organization part of the quota attainment? It is a problem if not. You will not get a channel partner sales team that is as motivated. I have scar tissue to prove this one.

Consider basing criteria on the following events:

a-Hunting

b-Customer success

c-Customer commitment-longer-term agreements

- Does the sales compensation plan fit the stage of the business?

- Account expansion in existing accounts

- Sales incentives-in place or not?

- Weekly reporting on sales and activities. Measuring leads created, leads worked, demos to customers.

- Not enough companies can adequately illustrate the value of making the journey up the pyramid to their prospective partner.

- Similarly, not enough companies have an accurate and robust understanding of their cost of sale for each level. (Hint: It goes down as you go up.)

- If a partner is not performing, move them out quickly.

"Relationship quality is the pre-eminent factor in predicting channel partner success. In short — the better the relationship, the better the results."

When your foot hurts, you are probably standing on your own toe... quote that applies to channel management.

" The greatest among us serves the most"-Steven Covey

Postscript-Partner sales and learning incentive.

The incentive needs to be structured to drive behavior and more business for your company.

Rewards, as we discussed, can be a weekend getaway with a significant other. I recommend an educational component for the weekend getaway and time with your team. The incentive can vary depending on the behavior you are looking to drive, the type of partner, and the strength of the partnership...

It can be a point-based structure - X points for attending your meeting, completing a learning event/module, new accounts, increasing revenue within a specific account, etc....

Once the partner or partner employee achieves a specific point level, they earn the trip.

Some more data is below:

A non-cash reseller sales incentive program can be a great way for a business organization to motivate its resellers and boost sales. Non-cash incentives can be more effective than cash incentives because they are more memorable and have a higher perceived value[1].

One example of a non-cash incentive program is an online reward catalog that features millions of rewards in ticketed events, travel, and merchandise categories[1]. These non-cash rewards carry personal significance and trophy value because your reseller incentive program participants select the rewards most appealing and motivating to them[1].

Another example is creating an annual incentive plan for non-sales employees by first establishing your target revenue for the year and setting that at 100 percent. Then assign a percentage of your employee's salary — 10 percent, for example — as the cash bonus[2].

Non-cash incentives that do require a financial investment can often be deducted as a business expense[3]. They spark intrinsic motivation, make people feel valued, give them room to grow, and show them the impact they make on the organization[3].

There are several benefits of using non-cash reseller sales incentives. Non-cash incentives can be more creative, personalized, and memorable than cash incentives[1]. They can also help you differentiate yourself from your competitors, as you can offer something unique or relevant to your niche or industry[2].

The emotions tied to non-cash rewards can overpower the simple usefulness of cash[2]. With non-cash sales reward programs, not only are your rewards more attractive and motivating you end up investing less to get that better return[2]. Non-cash incentives will also increase the perceived value of your services, as clients may feel that you are giving them something extra or special[1]. Furthermore, non-cash incentives can foster a stronger emotional bond and loyalty between you and your partners, as they may appreciate your generosity and thoughtfulness[1].

Meeting your resellers can also be combined with travel incentives to improve channel partner relationships[2].

Here are some tips for creating an effective incentive program:

- Identify your goals: Before you start creating an incentive program, you need to identify your goals. What do you want to achieve with the program? What behaviors do you want to encourage? What results do you want to see? Your incentive program should be aligned with your business goals. Make sure the incentives you offer are tied to specific behaviors or results that will help you achieve your goals.

- Know your audience: You need to know your audience and what motivates them. What do they value? What are their interests? What are their goals?

- Choose the right incentives: Choose incentives that are relevant and meaningful to your audience. Non-cash incentives can be more creative, personalized, and memorable than cash incentives.

- Set clear and measurable goals: Your goals should be clear and measurable so that you can track progress and success. Set clear rules and guidelines for the incentive program. What are the deadlines? What are the terms and conditions?

- Set clear eligibility criteria: Set clear eligibility criteria for the incentive program. Who is eligible to participate? What are the requirements?

- Communicate effectively: Communicate the incentive program effectively to your audience. Make sure they understand the goals, the incentives, and how they can earn them.

- Make it fair: Make sure the incentive program is fair and equitable for everyone involved.

- Make it timely: Make sure your incentive program is timely and relevant. Offer incentives for behaviors or results that are important now, not in the distant future.

- Make it visible: Make sure your incentive program is visible and well-communicated.

- Use multiple channels to communicate the program and make sure everyone knows how they can participate.

- Measure and track progress: Measure and track progress regularly to ensure your incentive program is effective. Use data to identify areas for improvement and adjust the program as needed. Evaluate the incentive program regularly and adjust it as needed to ensure it is effective.

- Celebrate success: Celebrate success and recognize participants who achieve their goals. This will help build momentum and encourage continued participation.

- Choose the right destination: Choose a destination that is relevant and meaningful to your audience. Consider their interests and motivations. They will love hanging out with you.

- Communicate effectively: Communicate the incentive program effectively to your audience. Make sure they understand the goals, the destination, and how they can earn the trip.

- Keep it simple: Keep your incentive program simple and easy to understand. Avoid complex rules or requirements that may confuse or discourage participants.

- Here are some common mistakes when creating an incentive program:

- Focusing too much on the reward: If you focus too much on the reward, you may lose sight of the behaviors or results you want to encourage. Make sure your incentives are tied to specific behaviors or results that will help you achieve your goals.

- Offering irrelevant incentives: Make sure your incentives are relevant and meaningful to your audience. Avoid offering incentives that are not aligned with their interests or motivations.

- Making it too complex: Keep your incentive program simple and easy to understand. Avoid complex rules or requirements that may confuse or discourage participants.

- Not measuring progress: Measure and track progress regularly to ensure your incentive program is effective. Use data to identify areas for improvement and adjust the program as needed.

- Not communicating effectively: Communicate the incentive program effectively to your audience. Make sure they understand the goals, the incentives, and how they can earn them.

- Not making it fair: Make sure the incentive program is fair and equitable for everyone involved.

- Not adjusting the program as needed: Evaluate the incentive program regularly and adjust it as needed to ensure it is effective.

- Lack of family and significant other support. Get the word out to those people about the additional rewards that personally impact the channel salespeople and it will accelerate your sales. Like adding another sales manager for your company.

Chapter 12

SUMMARY

This book and the timing of the publication is critical for those of us involved in revenue generation. The world has changed, and we need more tools and resources as a lifeline for our business and personal success. That is our mission and intention.

Follow the processes, stay ahead of the technology, and keep an eye out for more change. Subscribe to our newsletter, and we will provide the latest updates for you.

We wrote this book as a teaching tool for the many salespeople who find themselves frustrated with the traditional selling methods promoting product knowledge and a one-size-fits-all solution. Within that old framework, the salesperson is often flagged by the prospect as dishonest, slick, and at worst a liar. Yet so often it is the salesperson who is deceived or feels deceived by the prospect.

Our strategies for developing successful salespeople undo those old stereotypes. Understanding the selling process, learning to take control of the selling process, and mastering the steps to a successful sale provide a winning formula for both parties in a sale. The salesperson is confident that the money for his efforts will be in the bank, and the clients know they will receive a solution for their problem. The goodwill generated by two satisfied parties leads to a successful future in sales. We hope that in the end you will be a better listener, a better communicator, and a professional who realizes that what is hoped for in a sale is always that both parties win.

Bibliography

1. Bach, Richard. *Jonathan Livingston Siegel*: Avon, 1976.

2. Bandler, Richard, and Grinder, John. *Frogs Into Princes*: Real People Press, 1979.

3. Bandler, Richard and Grinder, John. *Using Your Brain for A Change:* Real People, 1985.

4. Bettger, Frank. *How I Raised Myself from Failure to Success in Selling*: Simon & Shuster, 1947.

5. Bosworth, Michael. *Solution Selling*: McGraw–Hill, 1994.

6. Buzotta, Lefton. *Effective Selling Through Psychology*: Ballinger, 1965.

7. Carnegie, Dale. *How To Win Friends and Influence People*: Pocket Books, 1936. 8. Hartman, Thom. *Cracking The Code*: Berrett-Koehler Publishers, Inc., 2007.

9. Hogan, Evin. The Psychology of Persuasion: Pelican Publishing, 1966.

10. Hogan, Evin. *The Science of Influence*: John Wiley & Sons, Inc., 2005.

11, Hill, Napoleon. *Think and Grow Rich*: Combined Registry Co., 1937

12. Jolles, Rob. *Customer Centered Selling*: Free Press, 2000.

13. Konrath, Jill. *SNAP Selling*: Penguin Group, 2010.

14. Kurlan, Dave. *Baseline Selling*: authorhouse, 2005.

15. Laborde, Genie. *Influencing With Integrity*: Dell, 1989.

16. Mandingo, Og. *The Greatest Miracle in The World*: Frederick Fell, 1977.

17. Meyer, Paul. *The Power of Goal Setting*: Success Motivation Institute, 1960.

18. Morgan, Sharon Drew. *Selling With Integrity*: Berkeley Press, 1999

19. Peale, Norman Vincent. *The Power of Positive Thinking*: Prentice Hall, 1952.

20. Rackham, Neal. *Spin Selling*: McGraw–Hill, 1988.

21. Robbins, Anthony. *Unlimited Power*: Free Press, 1985.

22. Robert III, Martyn. *Robert's Rules of Order*: Da Capo Press, 1876.

23, Stone, W. Clement. *The System That Never Fails:* Prentice Hall, 1962.

24. Wheeler, Elmer. *How to Sell Yourself to Others*: Dell, 1947

25. Wheeler, Elmer. *Tested Sentences That Sell*: Prentice Hall, 1935

26. White, Wendall. *The Psychology of Dealing*: The McMillan. 1936

Glossary

Ballpark range - the process of learning the minimum to maximum resources available to purchase.

Bandwidth - in business jargon, the resources needed to complete a task or project.

Buying Influencers – Individuals with decision-making authority.

CFO – Chief Financial Officer

CEO – Chief Executive Officer

COO – Chief Operating Officer

CRM – Customer Relationship Management

Charge Back – negative dollar charges against a commission statement.

Chauffeur - a person inside the prospects company who helps a salesperson through the selling process.

Commission Statement - statement of earned commissions.

Complex sale - a sale that has high dollar value and multiple buying influencers. Generally, has a long selling cycle.

Confirmation - confirming the sale with the customer.

Dominant Buyer - the principal buying influencer; can trump other buying influencers by saying yes or no.

Dynamic positioning statement - a short statement identifying the type of customers a salesperson works with, what specifically they do for their customers, and a third-party report about the results their customers experience because of using the salesperson's product or service.

Early Warning Indicator - signal from the prospect of problem to be solved. See Ch. 4

ERB - emotional reason(s) for buying.

EVP - executive vice presidents

GOLD - the potential value of the salesperson's products/services in the marketplace.

Investigative Buyer - the individual who researches products and services for their company.

Meeting Agenda – a written or oral agreement between the salesperson and the prospect(s) that defines the outcome of the sales call.

Moment of Choice – the point in the sales call that determines which party will control the sale.

Pre-Presentation Agreement – A review of all the factors influencing the sale. See Ch. 7.

Radio Silent – when the prospect(s) no longer communicates with the salesperson.

Resources – the amount of money available to purchase the salespersons product or service.

RFP - Request for Proposal

RFQ - Request for Quote

ROI – return on monetary investment.

Sensitive Buyer – the individual within a company most likely to suffer from the consequences of not having the salesperson's product/service.

Signing Authority aka Dominant Buyer – person who has the authority to sign the order.

Social Media – web-based and mobile technologies used to turn communication into interactive dialogue.

Terms - agreed-upon payment method.

T I O - Think It Over

VP – Vice President

Simple Sale – a low-dollar volume sale. Typically has one to two buying influencers and is generally a short sale cycle.

Solution – the answer to the Emotional Reason for Buying.

Utilitarian Buyer – the primary user of the salesperson's product/service.

Contact: http://www.seicasystems.com/

www.ingramcontent.com/pod-product-compliance
Lightning Source LLC
Chambersburg PA
CBHW050450290526
45786CB00006B/2234